For Fabiana Cuellar

Fabiana, may this book add to your marketing skills and your understanding of The Crosby way.

With best wishes for your success.

Ralph Crosby

October 2017

It's the
Customer,
STUPID!

LESSONS LEARNED IN A LIFETIME OF MARKETING

RALPH W. CROSBY

Ralph W. Crosby, Annapolis, MD 21401

Crosby Marketing books and tapes may be purchased at special quantity discounts for educational, business or promotional use. For information contact:

Ralph W. Crosby
705 Melvin Avenue, Suite 200
Annapolis, MD 21401
Telephone: 410-626-0805
E-mail: ralphcrosby@crosbymarketing.com
Website: www.CrosbyMarketing.com

Executive Excellence Publishing
1806 North 1120 West
Provo, UT 84604
Telephone: 801-375-4060
www.LeaderExcel.com

FIRST EDITION
Printed in the United States of America
10 9 8 7 6 5 4 3 2 1

$19.95 USA
Business/Marketing

ISBN-10: 1-930771-33-9
ISBN-13: 978-1-930771-33-8

Cover design—Ron Ordansa, Crosby Marketing

Acknowledgements

I owe a debt of gratitude to a lot of people who inspired me to write this book. Specifically, I want to single out my friends and mentors Tony Mikes and Os Guinness, who contributed directly to its content. Several of my colleagues at Crosby Marketing also contributed, especially the Internet specialist Fred Jorgensen, creative designer Ron Ordansa and PR specialist Gillian Pommerehn. My associate Claudia Eaton deserves a medal for keeping the manuscript and publishing matters on track.

My gratitude to my publisher Ken Shelton for his understanding and support. And a special thanks to my eldest daughter, Laura Crosby Avallone, for her professional editing assistance; to my son, Ray Crosby, President of our company, for his encouragement; and to my daughter, Belinda Crosby Butler, whose graphic talents appear in the book. Finally, let me acknowledge the contribution of my wife, Carlotta, for her constant patience and moral support.

Dedication

To my wife, Carlotta, and our children—Laura, Raymond, and Belinda—from whom I have learned a lifetime's lessons of love.

Contents

Foreword

I first met Ralph Crosby in 1990 while I was leading a seminar on advertising agency workflow efficiency. He came in, took his seat, and started taking notes. I had never seen anyone with the intensity of purpose he had in taking in all the information that I was putting forth. I had to assume he was serious about making his agency better.

That session led to a relationship that has now lasted nearly 20 years. Ralph's advertising agency, Crosby Marketing, had only 10 people when I first met him—it now has more than 50 employees. The agency's rise to be among the top marketing agencies in the country was carefully planned and based on very important and insightful marketing knowledge and practice, much of what Ralph describes in this book.

I believe I have played some small part in Crosby's growth and success. Ralph joined Second Wind, the advertising agency network I run, shortly after our first meeting, and we communicate regularly about a wide variety of issues, including the profound changes that are taking place in marketing today.

That's why I am pleased to write the foreword to this very important book.

Ralph and I share the opinion that marketing today is very different than marketing was 20 years ago. Back then, the marketer was firmly in control of the marketing process. Car companies, such as Ford or GM, essentially told the consumer what to think. Their advertising and marketing always proclaimed—Buy this! Try this! Do this! And their dealers and salespeople controlled the buying process, keeping select information secret and using that information as a bargaining chip to gain an advantage with the buyer. In other words, don't let the customers get ahead of you. Try to take advantage of them.

All of this has changed.

Now the consumer challenges the car company. Today's smart car buyers know everything there is to know about how to negotiate when buying a car; dealer costs, models available, their cars' value, etc.

Smart marketers know they cannot control their customers anymore. The internet has changed all that.

Today's consumers are very smart. They don't want to be sold. They want to choose. The old advertising idiom—the unique selling proposition—has been replaced with the unique buying proposition.

To recall my high school Latin: It used to be *caveat emptor*, "let the buyer beware." It is now *cave emptorem*, "beware of the buyer."

It is a known fact that today's consumers trust marketers less and their friends more. That's why the new social media has blossomed so quickly as not only a social tool, but a business tool as well.

All of this and much more is explored in Ralph's book, *It's the Customer, Stupid!*, a treatise about lessons learned in a lifetime of marketing. Ralph has done a great job of providing an overview of what 21st century marketing will look like, and how businesses need to adjust and adapt to the new realities. All of this in a well-written but casual style, filled with practical examples and real life experiences.

This is a book that will help you succeed in business by listening to the customer and joining in on the conversation, rather than trying to bludgeon people into buying your product or service.

Tony Mikes
Wyomissing, Pennsylvania

Preface

Lucky guy that I am, I have had three exciting and different careers in my life: First as a journalist writing for newspapers and magazines; then as a business owner/manager/marketer; and finally, for the longest period—more than three decades—as owner of one of the largest and most successful ad/PR agencies in the Baltimore-Washington, D.C., region. All of these careers have one thing in common: the need to communicate with an audience, whether to inform a reader, manage employees and sell to customers, or help a client move customers to action or change their behavior. In a sense, and we'll talk more about his later, all of this is marketing. In fact, Peter Drucker, the father of modern management, said in my favorite quote about marketing: "Marketing is much broader than selling; it is not a specialized activity at all. It encompasses the entire business. It is the whole business seen from the point of view of its final result; that is, from the customer's point of view."

When the staff of my ad/PR agency, Crosby Marketing Communications, grew to more than 50, I realized that the newer members didn't always have access to the concepts that had made us successful. So, I decided to pass along those ideas in short memos I called "Ralph's Tips." What evolved was a tapestry of best practices woven through years of experience and the wisdom learned from the masters of marketing. As I wrote these "Tips," I recognized that in each there existed a common thread—the customer. Focus on the customer had driven our marketing communications since I founded the company in 1973. That focus is the theme of this book and the reason for its title:

It's The Customer, Stupid!
Lessons Learned In A Lifetime Of Marketing

I've had clients tell me their business was driven by their products,

11

their management techniques, their personnel, or their technology. I'm sorry, but it's the *customer*.

The title came to me in the shower one morning (ideas, like songs, always sound great in the shower) as I prepared to go to work. "I'm sorry, but it's the customer, stupid," I said to myself. Of course, that phrase mimicked the words, "It's the economy, stupid!," that James Carville, Bill Clinton's political strategist, used as a central theme to answer the question, "What is the presidential campaign about?" This book seeks to answer the question, "What is marketing really all about?"

As you can see, I claim no originality in the title of this book. But neither can James Carville. His theme was a takeoff on such earlier expressions as the 1970s "KISS" advertising formula, which stood for "Keep it simple, stupid."

Nor was I the first to parlay Carville's theme into marketing, as I discovered during my research. In his book *The End Of Marketing As We Know It*, published in 1999, Sergio Zyman, noted marketing author and former chief marketing officer at the Coca-Cola Company, used a similar phrase and explained its relevance to marketing very well. He wrote:

" 'It's the economy, stupid' became the watch phrase of the (Clinton) campaign and a verbal model used by people everywhere. My version for marketers is:

'It's the consumers, stupid.' If you are in business and your goal is to maximize profits, as it should be, the only way you can succeed is by focusing on, understanding and pleasing consumers. If you don't do that, you will never be able to succeed."

Sergio Zyman, along with many marketing gurus of the last 50 years—unlike Mr. Zyman, most of them academics or theorists—have created a consensus on the ascendency of the customer's value in business. What I add is a perspective of the marketer who has seen that value in day-to-day operations—like the foot soldier on the front line executing the strategies formulated by the generals at headquarters. In this book, the reader will find the valuable lessons I've learned on the front lines over a lifetime of marketing. Whether my client was a small local restaurant or a giant, global Fortune 100 corporation, "Keep your eye on the customer" was always the battle cry.

For me, seeing that customer value began at an early age, as explained in the following introduction on the education of a marketer.

Ralph W. Crosby
Annapolis, Maryland

Prince Valiant and the Katzenjammer Kids

The Education of a Marketer

B eing from a family of modest means, making money was always a goal in my youth. From my snowball stand in summer at age 10 to selling groceries at the local meat market at 18 to help defray the cost of college, work was part of my education.

In between selling snowballs and sirloins, I delivered and sold newspapers. In the 1940s, on Saturday nights in my hometown, Annapolis, Maryland, the residents, farmers, and watermen would come to Main Street downtown, and several of us youngsters would sell them the Saturday night edition of the Sunday papers, *The Baltimore Sun* and, my favorite, Hearst's *Baltimore News-Post*. The latter undoubtedly appealed to me because, unlike the staid old *Sun*, the outer section of the *News-Post* was the colorful comics, not the front page.

Because I lived on Main Street, I knew most of the shopkeepers, and some would wait for me to come by with their paper.

I developed a "clientele" for the papers, from the genteel ladies in the musty Main Street hat shop to the proprietor of my favorite spot, the bustling pool room a block down the street, to the distant cousin who came in from the farm every Saturday night. Even at my young age, it became clear, through common sense, that I could sell my papers most easily to loyal customers.

Of course, it was not until many years later that I could give this "clientele" concept a formal marketing name—"brand loyalty." In simple terms, your brand is how your customers think and feel about you and what you offer. As we'll discuss later, creating brand loyalty can pay off over the lifetime of the customer.

After selling papers on Saturday night, I'd take home a News-Post and spread it out on my bed. I'd read the full-color comic pages first. My favorite strips were Prince Valiant and the Katzenjammer Kids. Next would come the sports pages. Once in a while, some news item would catch my eye, and I'd be fascinated by the story telling.

Hindsight tells me those Saturday nights helped fashion my two careers, as a journalist first, then as a marketer.

It's clear to me today that the latter career is a direct descendent of the former. The link is communication with a target audience. The value of one-to-one relationships and sales was a necessity in the days before mass marketing—think door-to-door salesmen, street vendors, and the corner grocer. It's a concept that has reemerged in the Internet age with its blogs, Facebook, Twitter, Flickr, and other social networks.

Write for the Reader

It was in my years at the University of Maryland College of Journalism that the importance of communicating with the audience began to be ingrained in my psyche. It was the feature writing prof who kept pounding into my head, "You're not writing for yourself, you're writing for the reader!" That message was buttressed at my first newspaper job—on the Baltimore *News-Post*—by the gruff city editor, who chastened me with, "Kid, you're not writing for yourself or for me. You're writing for the people who buy the paper. They're your customers." I was reminded of the ubiquity of that journalistic credo as recently as 2009 when the new Dean of Maryland's College of Journalism, Kevin Klose, was introduced to some faculty and supporters. Kevin, the man who built National Public Radio (NPR) into a media powerhouse and a one-time *Washington Post* Moscow Bureau Chief, spied in the audience Pulitzer prize-winner Haynes Johnson, also a *Washington Post* alum then on the Journalism College faculty. Kevin told how, when assigned to Moscow, a place he had never been, he went to the more experienced Haynes Johnson seeking advice on how to report about Russia to *Post* readers. "Find one person you want to write to," Haynes advised, "and write to him."

HAPPY SCHOOL DAYS
1946-1947

The author as a youngster—
around the time he was selling
newspapers and learned his first
lesson about customer loyalty.

Ralph Crosby, shown in the newsroom of the *Baltimore News-Post* (circa 1958).

The author shown leaving the
White House after a 1960s
press conference.

A Washington Correspondent, Ralph Crosby (left) interviews Robert
Kennedy in 1961.

Among Crosby's (left) many interviews conducted in Washington was one with the powerful chairman of the House Ways and Means Committee, Wilbur Mills.

Cover of *Kiplinger's Changing Times* magazine at the time Ralph Crosby was Associate Editor, and the cover of the his first book.

The Crosby Building in Annapolis, Maryland. Headquarters of
Crosby Marketing Communications.

Ralph Crosby, in the offices of his company, Crosby Marketing
Communications.

Person-To-Person Communications

As I succeeded as a reporter on the *News-Post*, the editors added various responsibilities. I joked that Hearst gave titles instead of raises. At one point, I was reporter, Book Editor and Industrial Editor, all at the same time. The latter title came in handy when I was offered a job as Washington correspondent with business magazine publisher Chilton Publications in 1960.

I went to work in D.C. when President Eisenhower was completing his presidency and John F. Kennedy was starting his, and an exciting part of the job was attending their press conferences. But the most enjoyable aspect of the job was interviewing government and business leaders for stories in *The Iron Age* magazine, the preeminent steel industry publication of the time, for which I held the title "Washington Editor." Among those I interviewed were Attorney General Robert Kennedy, Wilbur Mills—colorful head of the powerful House of Ways and Means Committee—and John Connor, who was Secretary of Commerce in Lyndon Johnson's cabinet.

John Connor, a lawyer and business leader active in politics, was influential in my early thinking about the importance of person-to-person communication. He once told me, "In a changing world, a changing nation, a changing industry, and a changing company, nothing is more important than human relationships." With Connor's words as a guide, I began to develop the concept that no matter what part of business was involved, personal relationships played a major role. In 1966, I gathered various *Iron Age* interviews and linked them together with commentary in a book titled *Person-To-Person Management*. As I explained the premise back then, "computers and scientific methods have revolutionized management. But in the revolution, when the human hand seemed most likely to lose its grip on management, the personal touch has pointed the way to success."

I had no way of knowing it at the time, but the book held the essence of what would be the driving force of my later foray into marketing. As I wrote in the book:

> *"The marketing concept which has evolved in recent years is based on the idea that all phases of a business must be customer-oriented. It means knowing a customer's needs and coordinating all departments— from research through sales—to serve those needs most effectively.*

"One major weakness caused by the lack of customer orientation is the failure to exploit opportunities suggested by the concept of market segmentation. This means looking at a market made up of diverse demands as a number of smaller homogeneous markets. These market segments have differing product preferences.

"Another weakness stemming from non-customer orientation is failure to understand the nature of products. The tendency to see products only as physical objects has been called 'one of our greatest marketing evils.' To be successful, the experts say, the marketing manager will have to think more and more of a product in terms of what the consumer gets out of it, less and less about what the maker puts into it. Management's marketing objective under this approach is not selling what it makes, but making what it can sell."

The book contained several expert opinions on which I could base those observations. One was Edward J. Green, an industrial marketing expert, who said, "The company must be customer-oriented rather than production-oriented. All company elements, from receptionist to shipping clerk, must be mobilized behind the marketing effort.

"Customer orientation is as important in industrial markets as it is in the consumer field. You must understand what buying habits are. Many women buy a brand of soap because they're interested in sex appeal. Industrial buying habits are different, but they must be known."

In *Person-To-Person Management*, Mr. Green was echoed by D.C. Burnham, then president of Westinghouse Electric Corporation. Mr. Burnham's approach for Westinghouse, he said, was "to organize the whole company from the customer backward. A company's success starts and finishes with the customer." A nice way of saying, *It's The Customer, Stupid!*

About the time *Person-To-Person Management* was published, I went to what would become my final position in Journalism. Armed with stronger writing credentials and a greater understanding of government, business, and finance, I joined the Kiplinger organization as Associate Editor of its magazine *Changing Times*, now known as *Kiplinger's Personal Finance*.

Kiplinger taught me quite a bit about marketing, especially because it had a unique publishing model. At that time, neither *Changing Times* nor the Kiplinger newsletters were supported by advertising, so subscriptions were the source of income. Therefore, Kiplinger became very adept at direct response marketing via television and direct mail. The direct mail letter Kiplinger developed was so good getting response that it beat all tests against it for almost 40 years and became the classic example of the formula for writing sales letters. (See the Kiplinger letter and discussion of the sales communication formula in Chapter VIII.)

From Journalist to Marketer

During my years at Kiplinger, my marketing chops were also honed by outside activities. For example, as campaign marketing director, I helped a friend get elected to the Maryland House of Delegates; I took on a few freelance public relations jobs to earn some extra money; and I became a paid advertising consultant to a friend and neighbor who owned Annapolis' most successful restaurant. That latter role changed my life.

The friend in question, George Phillips, had opened a small restaurant on the City Dock in Annapolis. The restaurant, called "Harbour House," grew quickly in success and size, and George had plans to open more restaurants. He wanted someone to handle marketing, PR, and administration and, in 1970, he asked me to join him in business. After much internal debate, the lure of business plus working in my hometown as my three young children grew up—and getting "a piece of the action," as George promised—won out over journalism.

For the record, we ultimately marketed six restaurants, in three of which I had a "piece of the action," two small shopping centers and, of all things, a wax museum. (More on the wax museum later, when we get to Marketing Mistakes.) I even bought a tennis club and a trio of tourist publications that presented walking tours of historic locales, Annapolis, Georgetown in D.C., and Alexandria, Virginia.

Needless to say, I had to learn a variety of marketing techniques for an array of customer types. As you can imagine, I learned the hard way, making my share of mistakes along the way. But I did learn some lasting lessons, creating a strong foundation for the advertising/public relations agency I founded in 1973, which later became my full time obsession—now known as Crosby Marketing Communications.

Before stepping into the business world, I shared my decision to leave journalism with a fellow Kiplinger editor, who gave me a priceless piece of advice. If you're going into the business world, he told me, you should read a classic book on management, Peter F. Drucker's *The Practice of Management*.

Peter Drucker's marketing wisdom, as expressed in that book, would influence every marketing maven to follow him, and it would give me a marketing mantra to follow. It was serendipitous, then, that years later I would be able to discuss this mantra personally with its creator himself, the famous "father of modern management," Peter Drucker.

CHAPTER 2

Lessons I Learned from Peter Drucker

―――――⊷◈⊶―――――

Development of the Customer-Centric Marketing Concept

I met the late Peter F. Drucker in 1992, in the midst of his efforts to instill his management principles in the nonprofit world. A colleague of mine, Bob Kramer, and I had been engaged by the Drucker Foundation for Nonprofit Management to promote its Self-Assessment Tool for Non-profits. Part of the promotion was getting Peter Drucker's ideas about nonprofit innovation on videotape. At the second of two video sessions, I chatted with Peter at the Aspen Institute's Wye Conference Center on Maryland's Eastern Shore, where he was attending a conference.

Despite his advanced years and innumerable similar interviews, he was still passionate about ideas, and he presented them forcefully. His voice was strong and still bore the accent of his Austrian heritage. In fact, he sounded a lot like another Austrian transplant, the bodybuilder-actor-politician Arnold Schwarzenegger.

Following the interview, Peter and I took a stroll in the Center's garden. I remember clearly that I wanted to let him know that his words had guided me in my marketing career, so I quoted him my favorite Drucker words on marketing. His response was instantaneous: "Practice of Management, 1954," he said, recalling the book and date the quote appeared. I half expected him to quote the page number. At the time,

Peter Drucker was 85 years old. Talk about "a mind like a steel trap." To remember that passage out of the 30 plus books he had written seemed to me a remarkable feat. It was also evidence of the importance this acknowledged "father of modern management" placed on marketing.

Peter added something like, "still good today." And I venture to predict that in the 21st century it will not change. I'll repeat the passage, which, in my estimation, should be a guiding principal for all marketers, managers, and business leaders:

> *"Marketing is not only much broader than selling, it is not a specialized activity at all. It encompasses the entire business. It is the whole business seen from the point of view of its final result; that is, from the customer's point of view."*

Remember, those words were written in the early 1950s when the foundation of marketing was "Sell the product."

The author (left) and Peter Drucker chat at the Aspen Institute on Maryland's Eastern Shore in 1992.

You get a hint of the foundation for Drucker's approach to marketing in a story he told about hearing a lecture by John Maynard Keynes in 1934 in Cambridge. "I suddenly realized that Keynes and all the brilliant economic students in the room were interested in the behavior of commodities," Drucker wrote later, "while I was interested in the behavior of people."

The behavior of commodities, i.e., products, and how to produce and sell them, was considered the purpose of business in the early- to mid-twentieth century, and some still view it that way today. But Peter Drucker turned that concept on its ear.

The author (left) interviews Peter Drucker at the Aspen Institute.

In *The Practice of Management,* Drucker posited that there was only one valid definition of the purpose of a business: "to create a customer." As he explained it:

> *"It is the customer who determines what a business is. For it is the customer, and he alone, who through being willing to pay for a good or for a service, converts economic resources into wealth, things into goods. What the business thinks it produces is not of first importance—especially not to the future of the business and to its success. What the customer thinks he is buying, what he considers "value," is decisive—it determines what a business is, what it produces and whether it will prosper."*

Because a business' purpose is to create a customer, Drucker concluded that the distinguishing, unique function of a business is marketing. Certainly others before him had suggested the importance of the customer to a business, but few had elevated marketing to such a lofty place in a business enterprise.

When you explore the argument for changing marketing from a product-centric to a customer-centric process, as I have, you realize that it runs from Peter Drucker through a number of major 20th century management theorists, such as the prophet of excellence Tom Peters, and eventually to the 21st century e-marketing pioneers.

Some marketing historians say the seminal expression of customer-oriented marketing came in 1960, with the publication of the late Theodore Levitt's article "Marketing, Myopia" in the *Harvard Business Review (HBR)*. In a 2004 reprint, the *HBR* editors saw the article as introducing "the most influential marketing idea of the past half-century: that businesses will do better in the end if they concentrate on meeting customers' needs rather than on selling products." Given Peter Drucker's words written in 1954, I would beg to disagree that Dr. Levitt "introduced" the idea, but he certainly gave it early and excellent expression in the *HBR* article and later in such books as *The Marketing Imagination*, in which (much like Drucker) he defined a business' purpose as creating and keeping a customer.

Dr. Levitt, perhaps remembered even more today for coining the term "globalization," was a legendary marketing scholar, Harvard Business School professor, and *HBR* editor. "Marketing Myopia" was indeed groundbreaking because it related the difference between selling and marketing to the successes and failures of major mass production companies and growth industries. "Mass production does indeed generate great pressure to 'move' the product," Levitt wrote. "But what usually gets emphasized is selling, not marketing. Marketing, a more sophisticated and complex process, gets ignored."

"The difference between marketing and selling," he continued, "is more than semantic. Selling focuses on the needs of the seller, marketing on the needs of the buyer."

Levitt explained in detail how such a misguided focus puts growth industries into decline, particularly because the product in question "fails to adapt to the constantly changing patterns of consumer needs and tastes." He suggests that management often develops a "dangerously lopsided product orientation," thinking of its company as producing goods and services, not customer satisfaction.

"The view that an industry is a customer-satisfying process, not a goods-producing process, is vital for all businesspeople to understand. An industry begins with the customer and his or her needs, not with a patent, a raw material or a selling skill," Levitt concludes. "The entire corporation must be viewed as a customer-creating and customer-satisfying organism."

I mentioned Thomas J. Peters in the line of management gurus championing customer orientation not only because his work may be more familiar to today's businesspeople but because he, himself, recognizes the wisdom of Peter Drucker. He does so in the landmark book, *In Search of Excellence*, he wrote with Robert H. Waterman, Jr., in which they find a corollary between America's best-run companies and customer orientation. In *Search*, published in 1982, there's a chapter called "Close To The Customer," in which the authors note that even in modern day management, some business people don't get the correlation. "Despite all the lip service given to the market orientation these days," they wrote, "the customer is either ignored or considered a bloody nuisance."

Peters' and Waterman's research found that excellent companies really are close to their customers, noting that "other companies talk about it; the excellent companies do it."

The customer-orientation concept has moved into the 21st century with a vengeance.

First, there was a new class of marketing gurus who came to the fore, led by Robert F. Lauterborn, a well-known marketing educator, Don Schultz, and Stanley Tannenbaum, the three co-authors of the book *Integrated Marketing Communications*. In 2000, I was fortunate to meet and hear Bob Lauterborn talk about what he called the new paradigm of marketing—*Cave Emptorem* (Beware of the buyer). At a meeting of agency leaders in the Second Wind Network of small- to medium-sized advertising and marketing companies, Lauterborn described the new paradigm this way: "The only sustainable source of competitive advantage is superior understanding of the customer."

To be customer driven, Lauterborn told us, you must maintain a focus on the needs and expectations (both spoken and unspoken) of customers, (both present and future) in the creation of the product or service provided. It was Lauterborn who also turned marketing ideology on its head by eschewing the traditional 4Ps of marketing for what he calls the 4Cs:

- Forget Product. Study <u>Consumer</u> wants and needs. You can no longer sell whatever you can make. You can only sell what someone specifically wants to buy.

- Forget Price. Understand the consumer's <u>Cost</u> to satisfy that want or need.

- Forget Place. Think <u>Convenience</u> to buy.

- Finally, forget Promotion. The word now is <u>Communications</u>.

Lauterborn was speaking to us at a time when the world was on the cusp of the explosion of online or e-marketing, which has taken customer contact to a whole new level. The evolution of e-marketing is not about Internet technology or applications. Neither is it about the growth of social networks, though they have become useful communications tools. It is about personal contact with the customer led by the customer, as we'll explore in detail in later chapters.

The Internet has lessened marketing's focus on seeking and selling to customers and has become more about customers seeking the seller. Today the Internet has become a vehicle for customers to find their desired products or services with a few clicks of the mouse and seek the best deals in the process. More and more customers use the Internet to make informed purchase decisions and to fulfill their need for value. Some of today's marketing specialists have recognized that.

For example, it's a basic premise of the book *Building Brandwidth— Closing The Sale Online*, published in 2000 by noted marketers Sergio Zyman and Scott Miller, in which they explain "making, strengthening and sustaining the connection to target customers—that's what building brandwidth is all about."

"On the Net, customization rules," Zyman and Miller explain. "Internet companies accept a key principle ignored by many other marketers: Fixate on the customer, not on the product or the competition."

So the Drucker principle of customer-centric marketing continues to thrive, even though—as Theodore Levitt, Tom Peters and Sergio Zyman each in his own time has pointed out—the customer is still often ignored as the key to business success.

Product orientation persists. For example, a Harvard Business Review article on "Reinventing Marketing," in the January-February 2010 issue, reported that "boards and C-suites still mostly pay lip service to customer relationships, while focusing intently on selling goods and services."

From personal experience, I know that the customer often remains an afterthought. I can't tell you how many business leaders have come to me asking for help in marketing their products but, when I probe, they have a difficult time defining who their customer is and what that customer values and needs.

CHAPTER 3

Just Who Is Your Customer?

Building Profiles, Databases, and Relationships

In *The Practice of Management*, Peter Drucker declared, "The first step toward finding out what our business is, is to raise the question: 'Who is the customer?'—the actual customer and the potential customer? Where is he? How does he buy? How can he be reached?"

Putting aside the 1950s' use of "he" as the generic for both genders, the questions are just as relevant today. Yet, these questions often are missed by the novice marketer, or the novice approaches "customers" too narrowly.

I contend the organization has multiple "customers," *those whose satisfaction is key to the organization's success.* As traditionally seen, they are buyers of products and services. For nonprofit groups they can be contributors; for those offering public service, customers can be volunteers or those who need services; for associations customers can be members; for a hospital they certainly are patients, but they can also be the doctors. In this case, doctors are the kind we call "internal" customers, and these include employees, consultants, suppliers, and others who help an organization succeed.

Looking at it this way, I have always considered that "customers" can be synonymous with "audiences," "consumers," "clients," "stakeholders," and "target markets." Therefore, your "customers" may be such targets as government entities or the media.

Even among businesses of a specific type, say a department store, there can be a variety of buying customers, e.g., suit buyers, jewelry purchasers, underwear seekers. Airlines seek passengers, but the coach passenger and first-class passenger are slightly different types of customers. They're all customers, but they have different wants or needs. Depending on your type of organization, you may have to segment your customer base to meet its different needs.

How do you accomplish that?

The simple answer is "customer information." You must study your customers' needs, wants, and preferences to supply what they are seeking. This concept is sometimes characterized as the WIIFM approach, in which the customer figuratively asks "What's In It For Me?"

This is the classic example of the "customer-centric" rather than the "product-centric" philosophy. It is the customer, not the company, who decides what he or she will buy.

Marketing Research
Gathering information on what the customer prefers to buy requires marketing research.

I use "marketing research" rather than "market research" because I believe the latter is really a component of the former. Research purists would probably disagree, but to me market research looks at specific markets and measures their size and other characteristics, such as information about what people want or like or what they actually buy. It is the organized use of surveys, polls, focus groups, and other techniques to study these characteristics.

Marketing research, on the other hand, not only includes such market research techniques, but can involve many other elements in the marketing process. For example, the research might include internal company information, such as how the company has used its marketing budget or its marketing staff.

Often, the two terms are used interchangeably, but for this book, we'll use "marketing research."

Marketing research should start internally with the information you already have. For example, the classic business inventory—how many of which products have we sold—can tell the seller what its customers want to buy. If you have a service company, you should know which of your services are in most demand. In my agency, for example, it didn't take a rocket scientist to show us that as the 21st century dawned, the clients' demand for online marketing services was growing rapidly. Our response was to develop an in-house interactive department to meet our customers' need.

Another tool that we have found useful is talking to our employees and suppliers about what they're hearing from clients. While not very scientific, these "interviews" can yield valuable information, such as a tip from a media salesperson who told us of one of his advertisers was unhappy it couldn't get a specific service from its agency—a service my agency could supply. Needless to say, that dissatisfied company went on our prospect list, and it later became a client.

Of course, the best way to find out what customers or prospects want or need is to ask them. Using surveys, focus groups, one-on-one interviews, etc., you can periodically determine your customers' needs and react to satisfy them. These information-gathering techniques have a number of ancillary benefits:

- Keeping in contact and building an ongoing relationship with the customer.
- Discovering problem areas or mistakes you may be making.
- Creating sales opportunities.
- Building a customer database.

I learned the value of customer surveys early on in my marketing career. At George Phillips' Harbour House Restaurant, on the City Dock, in Annapolis, Maryland, I instituted a simple survey to tell us who our customers were, where they came from, and if they were satisfied with the restaurant and its service. (See figure 3.1)

To our Patrons,

To help us serve you better, we would appreciate your filling in the survey on the back.

Your name will be placed in a drawing for ten gift packs of Harbour House Wine and Champagne (a mixture of six bottles).

Thanks for your assistance and your patronage.

Your Host,
George Phillips

To join drawing, please fill in:

Name _____

Address _____

City _____

State _____ Zip _____

(See over)

To our patrons
To help us serve you better
we would appreciate the
following information.

Number in party?
Men _____
Women _____
Children _____
Day _____
Meal Period _____

Occasion, if any?
☐ Just eating out, no occasion.
☐ Business group.
☐ Birthday, Anniversary.
☐ To entertain out-of-town visitors.
☐ On a trip.
☐ Other _____

Driving time to this restaurant? _____ Minutes
Home zip code? _____
Did you leave for this restaurant from:
☐ Residence
☐ Place of Work or Office
☐ Shopping
☐ Hotel/Motel
☐ Other _____

How long ago did you first come to this restaurant? Or, is this your first time? _____
If this is your first time, how did you hear about us?
_____

In the past month, what local restaurants other than this one have you been to for an evening meal? (Exclude fast food)
_____
_____

What do you consider our specialty?
_____

What is there about this restaurant that you particularly like?
_____
_____
_____

What is there, if anything, about this restaurant that you would like to see us improve?
_____
_____
_____

How would you rate the service you have received from our employees?
_____
_____

Thank you
Your host,
George Phillips
(See over)

Figure 3.1

Such surveys had unintended as well as intended consequences. For example, in the early 1980s when the economy was recessionary, the surveys pointed out that less families and more couples were dining at the restaurant. Discovering that problem allowed us to change some of the overwhelming number of four-person tables in the restaurant to "deuces," thus getting more parties seated at the same time.

Such surveying can get much more complex, of course. For example, in 2009, Wal-Mart was polling between 500,000 and a million customers monthly by directing them to its website from its stores. This was part of Wal-Mart's effort to put marketing "at the forefront of championing the customer internally." As Wal-Mart executives explain, "Every store actually gets a significant number of customers to respond about their experience, and therefore, the data that we capture is valid store by store, and it is actionable, because precisely customers are telling us how did they feel about their individual store."

Getting actionable information has become easier as web-based surveying has come into vogue. In fact, you can purchase off-the-shelf survey tools for designing and analyzing questionnaires in-house or you can create web-based surveys with an online service company that will do such surveys for you. Their service allows you to customize a survey, have the company send and analyze it, and download the resulting data.

At Crosby Marketing, we have used both tools. For example, for one client, the local county health department, we used both to help evaluate materials we used in a children's health marketing program. To evaluate children's healthy eating, for which we had produced a "Healthy Eating" kit, we surveyed parents who received the kit, using mail, e-mail, and phone calls. The data was entered into the off-the-shelf web-based tool we had purchased, and we were able to aggregate and cross-reference the results. To evaluate a more general "Healthy Kids Kit," we used an online survey service called SurveyMonkey.com.

Either way, simple or complex, such surveys can tell you just who your customers are. And the more you know about them the easier it is to get new customers like them.

Building Profiles

Organization leaders who *assume* they know who their customers are do themselves a disservice. Don't assume anything. Do your homework. Build an accurate profile of your customers.

A profile or customer biography will not only help you make better business decisions and make your marketing more effective, but it will give you information to find similar customers to target.

Customer research builds such profiles. Surveys allow you to track the customers' demographics—age, gender, income, education, etc; determine their geographic location; and understand their psychographics or lifestyle elements that reveal personal traits and behaviors.

You also can profile customers by other key elements, such as shopping habits and media usage. What type of products or services do certain customers buy, when, where, and how much? In what media do customers read or hear about offerings such as yours? Have they used your website for information, or have they searched the Internet for offerings similar to yours?

In my early days in marketing, gathering customer information was a laborious, paper-based process. I recall trying to determine buying habits of customers for an old-time lumber company that didn't keep separate records of most customers. Until we were able to get a customer counter survey going, we were limited to searching billing records and credit card vouchers. We were concerned that this information would be skewed because many of the company's individual customers paid cash. It was useful, however, to gather information about its business customers, such as builders.

Building a Customer Database

In those days, we tallied surveys by hand and kept the records in file drawers. The advent of the personal computer simplified and enhanced the process. The computer became an electronic filing cabinet. Today we do many of our surveys online and build customer profiles in databases.

Database software allows you to store customer information in segmented fashion in various compartments or "fields." For example, my company's database is segmented by type, i.e., client, prospect, VIP, media, friends and family, as well as the standard fields of name, address, affiliation, title, phone, fax, and e-mail. By entering the information in fields, you can manipulate it as you please. You can even add such personal information as birthday, spouse's name, dining preferences, or business-related data involving product or services the customer may want to hear about. The more information you have, the more ability you have to market to your customer one-to-one.

Database marketing is a computer-based way of creating and managing long-term relationships between an organization and its customers —known as customer relationship management or CRM. Companies use CRM processes, usually supported by dedicated, off-the-shelf software, to unify its customer relations and track customer information.

While handled through computer software, database marketing is not a computer program. It's a continuous marketing strategy designed to build relationships and harvest sales using customer data.

Who Is Your "Best" Customer?

The customer database enables you to continuously sell and cross sell to your current customers, and they are your best customers. Some marketers are so intent on finding new customers, they neglect existing ones. I have been told that it costs five times more to get a new customer than it costs to sell again or more to a current one. Whether or not that statistic is accurate, there is no doubt that obtaining new customers can be expensive—in both time and money—while existing customers already have shown some loyalty to your brand. Not only will that loyalty bring them back for more of what you offer, but they can be ambassadors for your product or service and create perhaps the best of all marketing—favorable word of mouth.

Speaking of ambassadors, there's one unique "customer" I'd like to single out for special attention. Perhaps it's because I've been singling this person out since I published *Person-To-Person Management* those many years ago. In this case, **it's your employee, stupid!** Talk about customers being "those whose satisfaction is key to the organization's success"! Employees are your ambassadors to your customers and the public. They can support your marketing efforts, or they can torpedo you. So, your first target for marketing is always your employees. They should understand your brand position and know what messages you are sending to customers so they can support your marketing efforts.

The employee will benefit, too. I'm reminded of words from *Person-To-Person Management's* preface, written at my request by W.F. Rockwell, Jr., President of the Rockwell manufacturing company:

> *"From one point of view, person-to-person management is a pathway to improved profitability. But, from another, the manager can help an employee find pride in his work; enjoy working for his company; discover outlets for his creativity and self-expression, and experience the feeling of dignity and worth as a human being."*

There's another unique "customer" that often gets short shrift—even animosity—from management, but who requires careful, positive, special handling because the benefits can be great. But, that's the next chapter.

CHAPTER 4

How to Handle One of Your Best Customers—The Media

The media are your "customers," so treat them like it. Cater to their needs. Build lasting relationships. Be honest. Forgive their trespasses, even though they won't always forgive yours. You have much to gain or much to lose. Believe me, I know; I've been on both sides of the relationship.

As a reporter, I wrote stories that praised and stories that pilloried, and as a marketer I've seen my clients both praised and pilloried. Sometimes they didn't rate the former and didn't deserve the latter. But, through it all, the one thing I learned is that if you treat the media as a customer, you'll get more praise than pain.

Why You Must Deal with the Media

Persons who have been burned by reporters wonder why they should try to work with journalists. To many, journalists are pests. They misquote you, sensationalize, and are rude and demanding, the thinking goes. Granted, journalists don't always get it right. But the fact is, you *must* deal with them, and here are several reasons why:

Journalists won't go away.

In fact, the more evasive a person is, the more persistent reporters get. Failure to talk with journalists results in one-sided stories and the impression that there is something to hide. Yes, you need to be concerned with image-building, but you also need to make sure that you are fairly represented in the media and that the public gets accurate, useful information. Take advantage of—rather than ignore—the opportunities to provide this information.

You need the media.
Journalists can be your friends. The media have often publicized programs and provided an essential information service about organizations such as yours. To maintain the cooperation of journalists when you need them, you must cooperate when they need you.

You get credibility.
A positive story in the media about your organization gives you third party validation. Even if the story originated with you, it's often viewed as unbiased reporting because it appears in print, on the air, or online. Sometimes, such publicity has more clout than paid advertising.

The fact is that most journalists are like Brian Williams, the NBC Television news anchor, who said in a 2008 *AARP* magazine article:

> *"Do I think what we do is important? There's no good way to answer that and not sound like a pompous stiff. I think it's important because people watch it. They are our customers. As long as they're watching us, I owe them the best job I can do."*

The public often develops its opinion of any organization through what it reads, hears, and sees in the media. For many, the media are their only source of news and information; therefore, it is tremendously important to develop good media relations skills, especially getting to know members of the media that cover your industry.

Building Media Relationships
Building relationships with reporters, editors, publishers, bloggers, etc., builds trust which, in turn, improves your chances of favorable media coverage. Of course, you must be a trusted resource as well. It's not a one-way street.

Journalists are human beings, with personalities, sensitivities, and a job to do. Work on building a professional, yet human, relationship with them. Try to get on a first-name basis. Know the position and responsibilities of your media contacts. Exchange thoughts, problem areas, and even disagreements when there's no hot issue going on. Show appreciation for their work when it's good. Discuss problem areas in a diplomatic but firm manner when there's been an error (see later section on "When The Media Gets It Wrong"). Work on building this relationship now, and the rewards will come later.

I do recall some definite benefits from good media relationships. In one such case, the late Ed Casey, the editor of the local paper, *The Annapolis Capital*, and I built a friendship over the lunch table and the poker table. Ed never printed any puffery from me, but he always would listen to my pitch. Many years ago, *The Capital* had a policy of not printing stories about contracts won or clients gained by local small businesses, such as mine and my clients'. The paper treated such stories as puffery until I pointed out to Ed that the paper did report contract wins by big government contractors in the area. I argued that local readers might be even more interested in what their neighbors' businesses were doing. Not only did Ed agree to run our new business news, but the paper started putting more emphasis on local small business.

The editor of a major metropolitan daily recently told my company's media relations director that "relationships can mean the difference in having your e-mail read or deleted. And be sure to talk to your contacts regularly, especially when you have nothing to pitch."

When a personal relationship is impossible because of distance, e-mail can be the next best thing. Reporters can check their e-mail in the office and out and can respond immediately, if necessary. However, some reporters may not like too much e-mail chatter, so try to discern how each likes to communicate. Some may like a phone call or the good old-fashioned paper news release, either mailed or faxed.

The News Release

The news release is the basic tool of media relations, often characterized as publicity or inappropriately called Public Relations. Media relations is but one tool of the broader discipline, Public Relations, which can include everything from promotional materials and personal appearances to press conferences and special events.

Publicity that appears in or on media is called "earned media" as opposed to advertising, the "paid media." The differences are critical in getting your message across to your customers. If you want certainty in delivering your message, advertising is your vehicle. It is predictable and relatively fast in producing results, but it's also relatively expensive. If you're looking for a more inexpensive option that has third party credibility, then publicity is your choice. However, it is unpredictable compared to advertising, which you can predetermine when and where it will appear, and publicity is relatively slow in producing results.

Editors like to receive releases in professional formats, which therefore give you a better chance of getting your release considered for a
story. (See the news release example that follows.)

Format, alone, won't get your release published. You have to have a
credible or, better yet, interesting story to tell to catch the editor's eye.
The media is bombarded with press releases and pitches, so yours must
stand out. Even in my youthful reporter days, the assistant city editor on
the Baltimore News Post would get a mound of press releases in the
mail each day and quickly sort them into two piles, a small pile of
"maybes" and a large pile of "nos." There weren't any "yeses" until the
"maybes" were checked for veracity and interest. I'm sure the same
thing is done today with both paper and electronic releases. Instead of
the trash can, the electronic "nos" of today just get deleted.

Media Relations in an Online World

Today, customers read news releases directly online. This means that
journalists aren't your only audience for releases. Instead, you're spreading your news to anyone with Internet connections and their search
engines, such as Google and Yahoo, which have millions of monthly
viewers who are looking for specific information.

So, your electronic news releases should be targeted directly to your
customers. Search engine optimization (SEO) ensures that your release
is easy to find. Therefore, you must use keyword phrases your customers would look for on search engines. Use these keyword phrases
for the main topic of your release and add these phrases to your body
copy. Also, be sure to link the release back to your website.

Your website should contain a media room or "news" section for
your latest releases and selected information journalists and other interested parties might look for. Besides new releases, the media room
might contain videos, photos, fact sheets, financial data, etc.

You should pitch stories to bloggers as well as mainstream media.
Some bloggers have vast audiences, including mainstream media
reporters who may find you on the blog. Also, find out if a targeted
reporter has a blog and be sure to read it and respond to it, if appropriate. In fact, major media often have electronic response mechanisms to
which you can send your ideas and opinions on news items. For example, cable news network CNN invites viewers to "join the conversation"
on its Facebook and Twitter pages and its numerous blogs. When the

news touches your organization in some fashion, such vehicles are a chance to send a message to the public.

A more direct way to get your message to the media is by responding to online chats by editors and subscribing to a query service from journalists. ProfNet, a daily query service from PR Newswire, sends journalists' requests for information out each day via e-mail or fax. You can respond directly to the journalist to see if you can add to his or her story. For example, my agency's media relations department responded to a ProfNet query from an editor at *VIVE* magazine, an upscale, regional lifestyle publication based in Florida. The editor was looking for products to feature in her breast cancer awareness guide. We sent her information on a pink ribbon charm produced by our client Pandora, a Denmark-based jewelry brand sold in more than 2,100 fine jewelry and gift stores across North America. The charm, which benefits the Susan G. Komen foundation, appeared both in a photo and story in the magazine, a win-win for us, our client, and the breast cancer foundation.

If your pitch succeeds, whether with a blogger, print journalist, TV reporter, or radio newsperson, being effective in your interview requires careful preparation. My years of experience as journalist and marketer taught me some lessons about how to deal with the media.

Tips for Effective Media Relations

It is not enough to simply be ready for an interview at the appointed time, armed only with a general sense of what you wish to convey to the reporter. Rather, your messages must be clearly organized, and what you plan to say should be carefully considered. These tips will help:

1. Prepare for the Interview

a. Be informed about the media—Pay attention to bylines (identifying the author of a story). When journalists call, it is helpful to know who they are and what stories they have produced recently.

b. Understand the media—The newsroom or studio scene is often a mad scramble for the story. The lives of most journalists are run by deadlines. Competition is tough. It's important to remember this when a journalist is bugging you. For example, a reporter may have an editor breathing down his or her neck for the story. It's important to give preferential treatment to journalists when returning phone or e-mail messages. Clerical support staff should be sensitive to the importance of a media call and consider pulling executives out of routine meetings to answer inquiries. Don't be afraid to ask journalists about their deadlines. This isn't just a favor to them. It ensures that you get an opportunity to give your side of a story before deadline.

2. Get the Facts

a. Obtain the journalist's name, affiliation, e-mail address and telephone number, and where he or she can be reached before deadline;

b. Ask what his or her deadline is;

c. Find out briefly what questions or issues they wish to cover;

d. Tell the journalist that you or an official spokesperson will call him or her back at an appointed time. Keep the deadline in mind and keep your word.

3. Learn Basic Interview Rules

a. *Always tell the truth*—This is more than an issue of ethics. If the media ever determines you are not being truthful, they will never let you off the hook. Your credibility suffers, and an otherwise positive situation is tainted or a touchy situation worsens. Additionally, do not exaggerate or embroider your story. Don't make the good news sound better than it is or the bad news "just a little" less bad. Reporters will consider these embroideries lies.

b. *Always answer the questions*—If you don't know the answer, say so. But, offer to find an answer—and do it. If you cannot answer a question, say why—proprietary information, confidentiality agreement, etc.

c. *Always know where you are going in the conversation and why*—Always know what type of media situation you are facing: Who is interviewing you, what they want to discuss, and for how long.

4. Communicate Your Message

Remember that an interview is a conversation, not a speech; however, it is important to have the points you want to make organized so you can discuss them in the order of their importance.

a. *Prepare a brief summary*—Before the interview, write a brief summary of the main messages—no more than three or four—you want to convey. This will help you remain focused on the important topics.

b. Note the interview length—Keep in mind the length of time planned for the interview. If the interviewer doesn't introduce your topic within a reasonable time, you can do so by asking a question that moves to the topic, or introduce the topic yourself. For instance, say, "One important topic/issue we haven't discussed is . . ."

c. Learn how to stall—Try to avoid long, uncomfortable pauses, rolling your eyes, or saying, "I'm glad you asked me that question." If you need to buy time in an interview, repeat the question, rephrase it, or discuss the history of the topic.

d. Be succinct—Keep your answers succinct, putting the most important idea at the beginning of the answer. Begin with your strongest point, then provide support. Don't over-generalize. Be specific, but not overly detailed or technical. Define terms that the general public may not be familiar with, especially if you're discussing complex topics. Avoid jargon.

e. Remain in control—Don't allow a belligerent or cynical interviewer to gain control of the interview. Don't be ruffled by questions or be put on the defensive. Politely correct misinformation and try to turn negatives into positives.

f. Avoid "no comment"—When you refuse to comment on an issue without any explanation, it is often perceived that you have something to hide. Instead of "no comment," explain why you cannot comment on a topic/issue at this time or indicate when you will be able to discuss the topic.

5. Respect Time Requirements

Time is everything to journalists. They work under constant deadline pressure in order to file timely news reports. To work effectively with the media, you must be conscious of their time constraints. For television interviews, arrive at least 30 minutes ahead of the scheduled time to allow for preparation. For radio, print, and online interviews, allow at least 15 minutes.

6. Learn to Bridge

The technique called "bridging" helps you control the interview. If you are asked a question that is not on your agenda, is hypothetical, or irrelevant, *bridging* is the effective way to respond. Usually when you bridge, you *first* answer the question, but answer briefly, concisely, and then move or bridge to what you want to discuss. These are some very simple bridges to use.

Examples:

- Turn "don't know" to "do know"—"I don't know the answer to that question. What I do know is . . ."

- Time shift—"Historically, that was the case. Today, here's what we're doing . . ."

- Emphasize positives—"That used to be important. What's important now is . . ."

- "No, let me explain . . ."

- "Yes, and furthermore . . ."

- "Yes" and "no" are the simplest bridges.

Other Quick Bridges:

- "The most important thing to understand about this is . . ."

- "The real issue is . . ."

- "What's even more important is . . ."

- "Let me put this in perspective . . ."

Here's a list of interview do's and don'ts. I suggest that you review it before talking to the media.

1. Don't say anything "off the record." Assume anything you say will be used.

2. Don't make any exaggerated claims or predictions.

3. Don't lie, mislead, or try to bluff the interviewer.

4. Don't say anything you're not sure about. It's OK to say that you don't know the answer, but offer to find out.

5. Don't use jargon or technical terms.

6. Don't look for the "on" camera. Talk directly to the interviewer.

7. Don't get angry and defensive.

8. Give your main point first in a concise, positive, *complete* sentence.

9. Be honest. Admit mistakes—denying them will only make you lose credibility.

10. Be as prepared and knowledgeable as possible.

11. Speak with conviction. Let it show in your words, face, and voice.

12. Choose the question. Journalists frequently ask several questions at once. Pick the question you like the best and answer it.

13. Watch or listen to the show, read the paper, or check the blog beforehand.

14. Refer to the host by name. Repeat the first name of on-air callers or other guests.

15. Say "thank you."

When the Media Gets It Wrong

Despite all your efforts, journalists sometimes get it wrong. They may leave a wrong impression, spell a person's name wrong, or provide inaccurate information. By being informed (reading news clips, watching TV news, etc.), you will know when they are wrong, and you can do something about it. Here's what to do when you think the public has been ill-served by information released through the media.

1. Check to make sure you did your job.

Were you responsive to the media inquiries? Did you provide accurate information? Before you complain to reporters and editors, make sure they can't counter by complaining about your own efforts.

2. Don't nit pick.

If a headline was only slightly misleading, or broadcast somewhat sensational, ignore it. It's a consequence of being in the public spotlight.

You don't want to become a nuisance.

3. Document your case carefully.

a. Call or write the journalist. This should remain private and serve the purpose of preventing a recurrence of the problem.

b. Privately call or write the journalist's supervisor. This should be done only after you've spoken to the journalist and received unsatisfactory results. Don't "demand" a retraction or equal time. Simply state the problem and allow the supervisor to choose the appropriate course of action.

c. Write a letter to the editor. This is for publication in printed media. It should clearly document the errors or expand on the previous story and explain your position.

d. Write a guest column, editorial, or response. Most media allow "counter-punch" type columns or reports, which are opinion pieces taking a viewpoint opposite to that of an editorial previously used by the media. Avoid asking too often. Blogs often allow for direct responses. And radio and TV may use your response as part of ongoing coverage.

In all cases, you should be diplomatic and courteous, but firm.

NEWS RELEASE EXAMPLE

FOR IMMEDIATE RELEASE
Contact: Ralph Crosby
ralphcrosby@crosbymarketing.com
410.626.0805

GET YOUR NEWS RELEASE NOTICED
Best Practices for Preparing, Optimizing, Placing News Releases

Annapolis, Md. (August XX, 2009)—In today's 24-hour news cycle, media are inundated with information. To break through the clutter and get your news noticed, guidelines for preparing, optimizing, and placing news releases were suggested today by Ralph Crosby, CEO of Crosby Marketing Communications, Inc.

-more-

Releases should have a clear, unique, and compelling news angle. Cut out flowery words and fluff. They should speak to media as well as the end consumer. Whenever possible, tailor releases to specific audiences and localize the news.

Create a targeted and inclusive media list of journalists who cover your news topic, and e-mail them the release. Strive to send out regular releases to maintain ongoing contact and build relationships.

Media targets may include radio and television news directors, editors or reporters at daily and weekly newspapers and magazines, and designated contacts at online media outlets. Consider e-mailing a condensed version of the release to appropriate bloggers. If the release warrants a large geographic and audience distribution, engage a newswire service.

Do your homework before sending out a news release. Know how the journalist prefers to be contacted; few journalists still request faxed releases. Be aware of media's deadlines: morning is typically better for most publications; late morning and early afternoon is better for television and radio outlets.

Be familiar with the media outlet to make sure your news is a good fit. Read the publication or view or listen to the news outlet.

Best practices for writing and optimizing effective news releases include:

- IDENTIFICATION: Provide a contact person's name, phone number, and e-mail address at the top of the page.

- RELEASE DATE: Most releases should be marked "immediate." Only stipulate a time if the news is "embargoed" until a specific date. In that case, alert media to the embargo by writing: "EMBARGOED Until [Date]."

- HEADLINES & LEADS: Creative, catchy, and gripping headlines and lead sentences are critical in capturing the media's attention.

-more-

• STYLE: Use summary lead (who, what, where, when, why, and how). Use short, punchy sentences with active verbs. Edit your work and be sure spelling and grammar are 100 percent correct.

• AT END: Put this ###.

An optimized news release will lead to increased online visibility and can help to generate ongoing publicity. To improve optimization, choose appropriate keyword phrases and try to use keywords three times throughout the release. Also incorporate the following best practices:

• SUBHEAD: Include a subhead in the release and use a secondary keyword phrase within it.

• LINKS: Add a link back to your website, as well as anchor text links throughout body copy.

• WEBSITE POSTINGS: Post the release on a unique page of a website and create a link to it on the website's home page. If possible, add social media tags on the webpage where the release is posted, e.g., delicious, Digg, Facebook, Twitter.

###

CHAPTER 5

How to Bond with Your Customers

Building Brand Loyalty

Nurturing relationships with customers—be they the media, employ-ees, buyers, members, etc.—is about building loyalty to your brand.

America's premier marketing professor, Philip Kotler, in the classic text *Principles of Marketing*, which he wrote with Gary Armstrong, defined *brand* as:

> *"A name, term, sign, symbol or design or a combination of these, intend-ed to identify the goods or services of one seller or a group of sellers and to differentiate them from those of competitors."*

To me, that sounds more like the definition of brand identity, the design-driven process that helps an organization develop a name, graph-ic, logo, colors, and design standards to give it a unique personality. When this image becomes widely known (think Nike's "swoosh") it dif-ferentiates the product or organization and creates value in the market-place. But it's not the brand; it is only a representation of the brand.

A brand itself is intangible. It exists in the mind of a customer as a pattern of feelings, associations, and ideas—the brand's attributes that customer has come to value through experience. It represents your promises to the customer. To give the brand credibility and appeal, the promises it represents must provide evidence that the organization is unique in a way that is meaningful and beneficial to the customer.

In exchange for that value, customers give their loyalty to the organization, its products or services. It demands a special relationship, or bonding, with the customer, one that satisfies the customer's wants or needs, practical or emotional. The value of this loyalty between customer and organization is called "brand equity." It is the monetary or activity result of having customers who are committed to the brand, and they often are willing to pay more, give more, or advocate more for it.

I learned the value of customer loyalty early on, as noted in chapter one, when regular customers always bought their Sunday paper from me. It was evident in my newspaper days as well, when the citizens of Baltimore were devoted to one afternoon paper or the other—*The Baltimore Evening Sun* or the *News Post*—with avid dedication. And in my days marketing restaurants, the diners who came back week after week showed me the value of having repeat customers over the long haul.

In the restaurant business I also discovered how that loyalty can erode through diminished customer service, reduced quality of meals or ambiance, or increased competition. Things can change quickly, so you must always be on the lookout for evolving customer wants and needs and how you fulfill them, all in light of competitive realities. As noted earlier, marketing research can help keep you in tune with your customers. We'll talk more about how to do that in the next chapter.

Consistency—Key to Brand Building

Brand loyalty requires repeated, consistent performance. Consistency with the customer is essential in building your brand.

- The quality of your offering must remain consistent. As Peter Drucker admonished:

  "Quality in a product or service is not what the supplier puts in. It is what the customer gets out and is willing to pay for. Customers pay only for what is of use to them and gives them value. Nothing else constitutes quality."

- Communications to the customer must be meaningful and consistent. Audiences today, bombarded by offline and online messages, have become resistant to some communications. Consistent representation of your brand is the key to remembrance, as noted psychologist Jarol B. Manheim wrote in his book *The Politics Within*:

"One way to increase the probability that this unconsciously received information will have some impact is to give it thematic consistency. That is, even though such messages may travel at different times over different media, they should possess a certain identifiable similarity with respect to both their substantive content and their format."

- Brand-building requires consistent positive contact with the customer. Personal relationships with customers will give you a competitive edge, but brand-building requires even more. You must concern your organization with the total customer experience, especially in the online marketing age in which the customer can *choose* to listen to your brand messages. So, whatever channels you use to contact the customer, e.g., online or offline media, in-store or in-person, your organization should be positive and consistent in satisfying the customer.

Remember our definition of customers— "Those whose satisfaction is key to the organization's success." Customers are the only things that really create value for your organization, so their loyalty is critical. The results of such loyalty are 1) repeat business with lower cost of sales than the expense of marketing for new customers; 2) unpaid ambassadors spreading your brand message; and 3) an ongoing value of the customer over the lifetime of your relationship.

America's Favorite Brands

If you think of your own purchases, memberships, and charities, you'll undoubtedly find organizations or products that have your loyalty. Among the standards in business you might use are Coca-Cola, Disney, and McDonald's. How can you avoid GE and its sub products?

Depending on your age, physical condition, or support of certain causes, you might be partial to such nonprofit brands as AARP, The American Heart Association, or the Special Olympics. And your online proclivities could lead you to use such brand leaders as MapQuest, Facebook, or Microsoft.

If you want to review some great examples of brand building, get your hands on *America's Greatest Brands*, which offers "an insight into many of America's strongest and most trusted brands." The loyalty garnered by the 57 brands—from AARP to Whirlpool—discussed in Volume IV of the book is truly remarkable. As explained by the publishers in the book's foreword:

"By far, the majority of these brands have been built upon a high-quality product or service, and have lived up to their promises and stood for something distinctive while generating considerable awareness. They define a clear personality and set of values and consistently remain faithful to their brand principles."

Within that statement you'll find the importance of consistency in quality, customer contact, and communications, our triumvirate of brand-building.

Among the many examples of customer-centric brands in *America's Greatest Brands* is Barnes & Noble booksellers. I choose this example because I am one of Barnes & Noble's loyal customers, among those who sit reading in the comfortable chairs sprinkled throughout my local store, or reading to grandchildren in the separate kids section.

You don't get much more customer-friendly than at Barnes & Noble, where the service personnel not only search for your book electronically but take you to the stacks to retrieve it, and where, as a discount receiving member, I get my extra bonus discount coupons by e-mail regularly. The company's mission statement aspires to such service, saying "We will not only listen to our customers, but also embrace the idea that the company is in their service." The company's adherence to that mission led *America's Greatest Brands* to conclude:

"By delivering on its promise of unparalleled service, selection, and convenience, Barnes & Noble is the booklover's second home. Practically every store and its contents are different because each store is an integral part of its community and neighborhood, reflecting local choices and tastes."

My local Barnes & Noble store even has a Starbucks inside, where you can have a latte or a meal while perusing your soon-to-be purchased or the store's reading material.

Speaking of Starbucks: While it is not in Volume IV of *America's Greatest Brands*, it has become a standard example of customer-centric branding. In fact, books have been written about its delivery of a *consistent* customer experience. In *The Starbucks Experience*, author Joseph A. Michelli writes:

"People flock to the company's stores for the total Starbucks Experience. In essence, people come into a comfortable setting where they are valued on a personal level and where a meaningful connection is made. Everything the company does is intended to give the customer a positive, perhaps uplifting, experience while purchasing a quality beverage or food item."

A Local Case History

I don't want to give the impression that only large, national companies can be brand-builders. Every organization can build a great brand. At Crosby Marketing we've helped many clients—from local banks and hospitals to area builders and associations—with successful branding campaigns. To give you an idea of how we do it, below is a case history of a branding campaign for Shady Grove Adventist Hospital for Children in the Washington, D.C., suburb of Rockville, Md.

Brand-Building Case History
"A Dog and a Hospital: Building a Brand Together."
Crosby Marketing Communications'Branding Campaign for
Shady Grove Adventist Hospital

OVERVIEW

For several years prior to 2007, Shady Grove Adventist Hospital (SGAH) located in Rockville, Md., in the Washington, D.C., suburbs, provided a high-level of pediatric care in its service area. With the area's first pediatric intensive care unit, first comprehensive "peds-only" emergency department, and a host of specialized services, SGAH had a growing reputation for pediatrics.

But with competition increasing, hospital executives felt it was time to leverage this strength and build a new "sub-brand" in pediatrics for Shady Grove Adventist Hospital, then a Crosby Marketing Communications client.

PLANNING

The program began with a multi-faceted research study designed to provide both a benchmark for ongoing program measurement and the information needed to inform the brand-building program. The research was developed in two phases to explore naming options and the creation of a brand icon. This icon would personify the hospital's character and help to create an emotional connection between the hospital and its primary target for pediatric services—children and their caregivers (parents and pediatricians).

Phase I: Naming
A series of focus groups were conducted with pediatricians and moms with young children at home. A short list of "most-likely" names was created from the groups and further tested in a quantitative telephone survey.

Phase II: Brand Icon Development
The second phase of research focused on the needs, perceptions, and attitudes of the primary recipient of pediatric services—children. In addition, a seamless methodology allowed us to gauge reactions from moms. This research required three steps: 1) Creative Discovery, 2) Brand Icon Development, and 3) Brand Icon Testing.

The Creative Discovery step involved interactive discussions and creative explorations with several groups of 5-6 children, a moderator, and an illustrator. The findings were then used to develop nine brand icon concepts. These brand icons were then tested with children and parents through interviews and brief written surveys.

Our objectives were clear—to develop a fully integrated marketing communications program to:

- Launch the new pediatric brand, building top-of-mind awareness and familiarity with the unique "hospital within a hospital."

- Introduce our newly selected brand icon.

To achieve these objectives, we did an evaluation of the following target audiences: Caregivers, both parents (primarily moms) and pediatricians; children; SGAH medical staff, nurses, employees; and the media.

RESEARCH RESULTS
The name selected from research was "Shady Grove Adventist Hospital for Children." One icon emerged as being the most appealing and having the strongest emotional connection with the hospital. A young golden retriever, "Sunny," offered both children and their parents a sense of comfort, safety, trust, loyalty, compassion, and warmth—attributes that mirrored the hospital's established brand character.

THE CAMPAIGN

The hospital became a critical point of brand reinforcement for patients, parents, and providers. On the pediatric floors evidence of Sunny was everywhere. Paw prints could be seen along the hallways, Sunny murals were done in every pediatric unit, one-of-a-kind Sunny stuffed animals were developed and were given to every child admitted to Shady Grove Adventist Hospital for Children. Even a life-size mascot was created.

Caregivers were given lanyards and badges with images of Sunny. Patient gowns were created with images of Sunny and Sunny stuffed animals were sold in the gift shop.

A children's storybook was developed where Sunny takes kids through a mini-tour of the hospital. The book also included a clever game designed to make the experience fun for kids. A version of the storybook was made available online as an interactive game for kids. The book was sent to every residence in the hospital's primary service area with children at home. The book was also promoted in local print advertising and through the hospital's quarterly newsletter.

A press conference was held at the hospital. At the event, our Sunny mascot took local media through the Sunny halls to experience firsthand the kid-friendly environment.

The Shady Grove Adventist Hospital for Children is featured in the SGAH's quarterly newsletter, *HealthAdvisor*. In the newsletter, Sunny has a regular column. Children have the opportunity to e-mail Sunny with questions, which he answers in his column, "Sunny's Corner." Kids can also send in pictures of themselves with Sunny.

EVALUATION

The overall campaign for the Shady Grove Adventist Hospital for Children was a tremendous success due in large part to the creation of Sunny.

• According to the hospital, advertising and direct mail programs generated hundreds of calls for information and requests for Sunny materials.

• Shady Grove Adventist Hospital reported that inquiries and referrals for pediatricians tripled after the launch of campaign.

- Local schools contacted Shady Grove to develop partnerships and events featuring the hospital's medical staff and Sunny.

- Medical staff reported that patients asked for Sunny when they entered the hospital.

- Physician satisfaction with the hospital and its marketing efforts reached an all-time high.

That's satisfying a lot of different "customers."

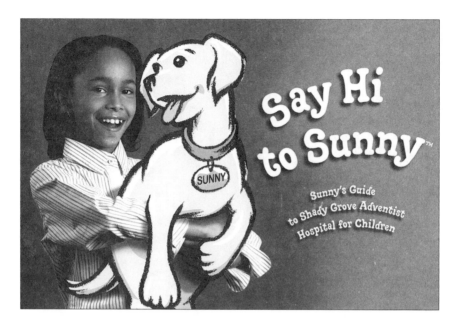

Tools of the Brand-Building Trade

As you can see from the case history, it took many marketing tools to help build the brand—including marketing research, audience targeting, brand identity creative, and advertising and public relations techniques such as media relations, newsletters, direct mail, affinity group partnerships, and employee involvement.

Employees are so important because they bring the brand to life. Whether it's a salesperson, an account person, or the CEO, in personal or business contact with the customer, they deliver the brand experience. And the deeper the relationship is, the deeper the loyalty goes. I say "personal or business contact" because the customer's experience involves many business activities; it includes service or maintenance matters, delivery of the product or service, billing issues, etc. As noted in Chapter III, customer relationship management or CRM is a data-based, computerized way of managing these relationships.

The computer, of course, has changed relationship marketing, allowing for one-to-one contact via the Internet. As we'll discuss in later chapters, brand-building on the Internet requires special marketing skills to turn that one-to-one contact into customer satisfaction and the loyalty such satisfaction can invoke. However, as the Shady Grove Adventist case history shows, there are techniques for brand-building that require attention to traditional, offline expertise. Over the years, we have developed specific best practices in marketing that facilitate bonding with the customer and creating brand loyalty. The next chapter will cover their evolution and execution.

CHAPTER 6

'Hear Thy Customer, Obey Thy Customer'

Best Practices in the Customer-Centric Creative Process

A s you can plainly see, everything in marketing comes together in a universe around the customer. But it's not a "big bang" universe where the stars and constellations form through explosive chance. The patterns of marketing and its management are basically systematic, consistent, and repeatable. Marketing is much more science than art, though art certainly is present in the execution of the creative side of communications. If we think of "science" as a skill reflecting the application of facts or principles in a particular branch of knowledge, then marketing certainly fits that definition.

The proof of marketing's scientific nature can be found throughout the 700-page basic text *Principles of Marketing*, by noted marketing educators Kotler and Armstrong. The book discusses the application of principles and processes to every facet of marketing: from consumer behavior and marketing research to market segmentation and measuring demand, from competitor analysis to communication and promotion, and everything in between. The book was crucial for me because within it I found the proof for the process I had developed through experience. That process was simple: Do your homework before designing and executing a communications campaign, and check it later to make sure whether or not it is working.

Best Practice #1: Strategic Marketing Process

That proof was the Kotler-Armstrong definition of marketing management as "the analysis, planning, implementation, and control of programs designed to create, build, and maintain beneficial exchanges with target buyers for the purpose of achieving organizational objectives."

It was the definition of the process on which I had built a business. This was the "strategic marketing process," one of two best practices I wrote about, talked about, and used with clients. I'll discuss best practice number two—Integrated Marketing Communications—later in this chapter. For me, the strategic marketing process consisted of four steps, and it almost mirrors the Kotler-Armstrong definition of marketing management. The four steps are followed in sequence until the process is begun again. Here are the steps, with the Kotler-Armstrong defining words in parentheses:

Step 1 (Analysis) Research and Analyze—The analytical stage of information gathering.

Step 2 (Planning) Plan and Decide—The decision-making stage of marketing.

Step 3 (Implementation) Develop and Implement—The marketing action stage in which the plan is executed.

Step 4 (Control) Measure and Modify—The checking stage where systematic assessments are applied.

The strategic marketing process doesn't end there. It keeps repeating, retracing the steps once more as the market changes and programs mature.

While I developed my version of this process before reading The *Principles of Marketing*, others had figured it out in even more detail. You'll find it in other marketing texts and other agency philosophies. In my experience studying other agencies, I have come across similar step-by-step processes. For example, the Baltimore agency Richardson, Myers and Donofrio (now Carton Donofrio Partners) espoused a five-step methodology it called the "P" process:

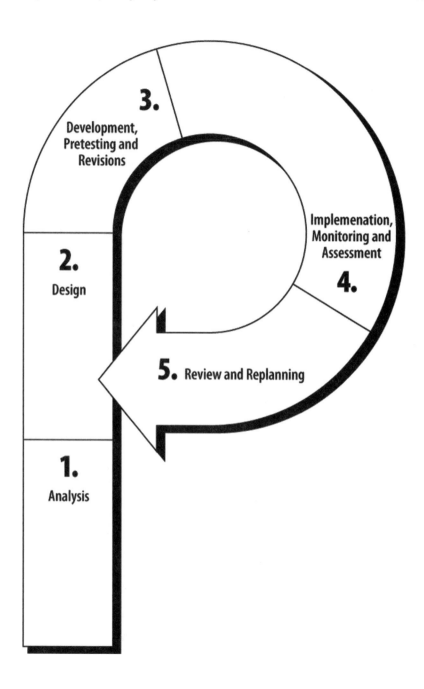

Years ago, William D. Novelli, co-founder of the global public relations firm Porter Novelli, used a similar approach with six steps, which he diagrammed as follows:

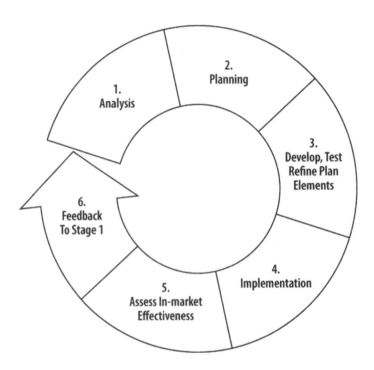

While slightly different in their steps, each approach starts in the customer's universe. The research and analysis in step one focuses on the customer. As noted in Chapter III, this is the stage in which you gather customer information, start building customer profiles, and create a customer database. Most important, this is the time to listen to your customers. Peters and Waterman, in research for their book *In Search of Excellence*, discovered that "the excellent companies are better listeners." They also discovered that these top-performing companies had a special way of being close to the customer. They were surprised by what that closeness did for these companies, noting: "They get the benefit from market closeness that for us was truly unexpected—unexpected, that is, until you think about it. Most of their real innovation comes from the market."

Thus my chapter heading, "Hear Thy Customer. Obey Thy Customer," commandeered from marketing prophet Robert Lauterborn and his co-authors. They called the new marketing paradigm, started in the 1990s, the age of "empowerment." "Empowerment means people not only choose what they wish to listen to," they wrote, "but also that they talk back and have the means to make themselves heard; wise rulers, those who keep their heads, hear and obey…."

Those words come from the book *Integrated Marketing Communications*, which is also the title of my second best practice. Like developing the strategic marketing process, our integrated marketing communications approach came out of experience. It developed at the confluence of customer need and customer feedback.

Best Practice #2: Integrated Marketing Communications

In the restaurant marketing research I did at the start of my marketing career, I usually asked the question, "How did you hear about the restaurant?" I noticed that many customers responded with several sources—"Saw your brochure." "Read a newspaper article about you." "Saw your ad." "A friend recommended you."

It occurred to me then that customers seemed to be impacted through multiple communications channels, and those customers were more apt to be regulars. They had developed a loyalty for one reason or another, and consistent communication appeared to be an important reason. (Later research was to prove that shared advertising images and messages spread across several marketing techniques created more awareness, interest, and purchases among customers.)

Of course, my early experience was in the heyday of the concept known as the "marketing mix," defined as a blend of controllable marketing variables that produces the right customer response. The marketing mix is not just about communication. It's about influencing demand for your offering in the traditional marketing concept known as the "Four Ps:" product, price, place, and promotion. These are the "Four Ps" that Bob Lauterborn called passé, to be replaced by "Four Cs," Consumer wants and needs; Cost to satisfy those wants and needs, Convenience to buy; and Communications.

Whatever you call it—promotion or communications—it didn't take a genius to see how the power of blending different techniques could have more impact on the customer and his needs. It was responding to customers' needs that sealed for me the concept of *integrated marketing communications*.

When I started my company, we billed ourselves as a public relations agency, but our small clients forced us into offering various communications techniques because they couldn't afford separate agencies for different methods of marketing. My entrepreneurial spirit also had something to do with it. When the client asked for direct mail, we answered, "We can do that." When the client wanted in-store promotion, we learned fast about that. When the client wanted marketing research, we studied all the research methods. The idea that we can fulfill whatever marketing communications the client wants or needs continues today, as Crosby Marketing has built an interactive capability staffed by experts in web and social marketing. I have always followed a premise based on the French Foreign Legion's motto, "March or die." My business motto, which my staff's sick of hearing, is "Grow or die." A business that does not change with the wants or needs of its customers cannot sustain success.

So, we practiced integrated marketing communications long before the term became fashionable. We always saw it as making all marketing communications work together as a unified force, rather than permitting such techniques as advertising, PR, sales promotion, and direct marketing to work in isolation. This maximizes the impact of the messages on the customer's mind. It's an example of the numerical definition of synergy, $1+1=3$, i.e., the sum is greater than its parts. It's also an example of thematic consistency being a key to remembrance. Originally, I defined integrated marketing communications as a means of making all of your communications speak with one voice to guarantee your message gets through to your target audience. But I've come to realize that definition is too limiting.

The definition used in the Integrated Marketing Communications curriculum at Northwestern University goes a step further, calling it, "The process of managing all sources of information about a product/service to which a customer or prospect is exposed that behaviorally moves the customer toward a sale and maintains customer loyalty."

Including "all sources of information" gives it a broader scope. The definition from the American Marketing Association is even broader and even better. It calls integrated marketing communications "a planning process designed to assure that all brand contacts received by a customer or prospect for a product, service, or organization are relevant to that person and consistent over time." The combination of the terms "planning," "brand," and "consistent" with "customer" describes integrated marketing communications' holistic approach to marketing.

The holistic approach should involve more than marketers. Business functions such as sales, finance, and distribution must work with marketing to ensure that they are consistent in customer contacts and communications. All too often, such functions go their own, separate ways, sending conflicting messages to customers. Some companies have solved this problem by using cross-functional teams to work with the marketing department and the outside marketing agency on client segments. My agency has facilitated it by involving a client's key executives and managers in the strategic marketing process so that in the end, we're all on the same page.

So, you can see how we arrived at two key best practices in marketing. In most cases, we have used them together in client campaigns. But in recent years we realized that what we should do, to differentiate our agency, was to put these two practices together, literally, in one proprietary methodology.

Getting at the C O R E of Marketing

Since we believed these best practices were the "core" of managing and executing marketing, what better way to brand it for my agency. Since it was an extension of our original four step strategic marketing process, the four letters of CORE fit well. In one sense it was easy. All that we had to do was fit words to the letters. On the other hand, we had to ensure that the process coalesced around the execution of integrated marketing communications. It was easier to do it than to explain it. But, as you can see in the following graphic and the explanation that follows, we successfully married the two practices in words as well as in fact.

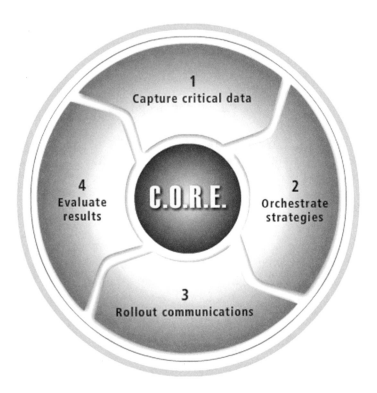

Like its predecessor process, CORE is a step-by-step guide that evaluates the relevance of the client's brand promise, defines target audiences, establishes key messages, shapes an integrated communications plan, establishes integrated tactics, and measures results. We've seen this process bring order and efficiency to marketing efforts, maximizing the odds for achieving clients' goals and objectives. One such example of the process in action was our national public education campaign for The National Association of Social Workers, as seen in the case history at the end of this chapter.

The first step—Capturing Critical Data—is the same as the old process—Research and Analyze. Here you must gather information to understand your customers, their wants and needs, and what your brand promises them. That understanding includes examining the competition and the structure within which the organization must operate, including its financial and personnel resources. This examination is often called a "situation analysis." Most times it includes a SWOT analysis, an assessment of strengths, weaknesses, opportunities, and threats. The perspective gained in this phase will drive everything else in the process.

The data collected and analyzed in the first stage now serves as a basis for step two—*O*rchestrating strategies, the planning and decision-making stage. This stage includes five broad areas: establishing objectives; developing marketing strategies; creating brand messaging; establishing tactics and the marketing mix; and developing an integrated marketing plan. The plan should create a seamless program that will connect the brand with the customers in a unified manner. While all five strategic areas are important, creating brand messaging is especially critical. It's the basic element of how your brand connects with the customer. Brand messages are the transmitters of consistent, meaningful communications, one of the three legs of our marketing stool. Without it, the stool will not stand.

With the plan as a guide, it's time to *R*ollout integrated communications—the marketing action stage. Here each component of the communications mix is developed and tested. The components of the mix, be they advertising, PR, interactive, etc., are all considered in light of the brand. The organization is integrated into the program. To influence today's customer, you must deliver a clear, consistent message on behalf of the product, service, or organization no matter what techniques you use and who in the organization uses them. Conflicting messages, delivered through a variety of techniques or personnel, will either confuse or be rejected by the customer.

As the implementation proceeds, you must *E*valuate results—measure and modify. Systematic assessments of available data are applied: 1) to determine the degree to which the marketing program is meeting its objectives; 2) to determine mid-course corrections in the program that may be required to address deficiencies or capitalize on new opportunities; and 3) to determine how to re-plan the next cycle of the process.

As noted earlier, the process keeps repeating. There can be no let up. Why? Because the customer's wants and needs change. Programs enter phases of decline, and the organization can change, as well.

As Lauterborn, Schultz, and Tannenbaum explain in their book: "We as marketers develop communications programs. The consumer responds. We get information on the response. We adapt to the customer's or prospect's communications wants or needs and begin the cycle all over again. It is integrated marketing communications that develops a win-win situation for the marketer and the customer or prospect."

Case History

"Help Starts Here"—From Marketing Process to Integrated Campaign
Crosby Marketing Communications' Campaign for the National
Association of Social Workers

OVERVIEW
Undervalued. Underappreciated. Underpaid. That was the plight of
social workers, which number more than 600,000 professionals. With
declining enrollments into the social work field and continued negative
press coverage, the National Association of Social Workers (NASW)
called on Crosby Marketing Communications to develop a branding
strategy and a National Public Education Campaign to change misperceptions of the social work profession and to broaden the understanding
of who could benefit from the help of a social worker. Crosby
Marketing followed its CORE process.

1. Capturing Critical Data
Crosby Marketing, working with NASW and an outside research
partner, conducted several types of research, including:

- Leadership sessions with selected NASW board members and
  NASW associates to discuss potential target audiences, campaign
  objectives, and positioning thoughts.

- Secondary research and media audit to review existing research
  studies, audit recent press coverage of social workers and examine
  similar campaigns.

- In-depth, one-on-one interviews with 12 opinion leaders to gather
  input and campaign ideas.

- Focus groups with the general public and social workers in three
  cities to assess awareness and attitudes towards social workers and
  to test message concepts.

The research spoke loud and clear: While misperceptions exist that
social workers only work with child welfare and only serve poor and
underserved populations, social workers are viewed positively as "helping" professionals. Still, few understand the breadth and depth of the
important roles they play and education credentials they require.

2. Orchestrating Strategic Planning

Based on the research findings, these audiences and objectives were established:

Target Audiences:
• Primary: General Public— "Sandwich Generation"
  ○ 35-54, female skew with children and aging parents
  ○ Parents to their children and caregivers to their parents
  ○ Could need the help of a social worker most

• Secondary:
  ○ Media, who need to be educated about the breadth and depth of social work
  ○ Social Workers, who need to be united under a consistent message

Objectives:
• To bring to life the campaign promise, "Help Starts Here," that was developed from the research.
• To educate the Sandwich Generation about the depth and breadth of social work practice.

Strategies:
• To change perceptions about what social workers do and who they serve, and at the same time, reinforce their professionalism.
• To demonstrate the depth and breadth of social work by providing deeper information on the five social work practice areas, along with real-world stories.

Using direction from the research, Crosby Marketing developed a clear brand position to communicate that social workers are the gatekeepers to turn to when solving life's complex issues. Hence the campaign theme: Social Workers. Help Starts Here.

3. Rollout of Integrated Campaign

A broad array of integrated communications strategies and tactics were used to carry the message across the country. A new logo and tagline were developed to represent and position the profession.

Social Workers
Help starts here.

A marketing video was also created to educate and inspire social workers in 56 NASW chapters to support the campaign and become better self-advocates. Crosby Marketing recommended and created the first-ever Social Workers website (www.helpstartshere.org) to educate consumers on key topics and make it easy to locate a social worker in their communities.

To demonstrate how social workers help, a number of real stories were profiled on the website. These stories detail a "turnaround" or how lives have been changed through the help of a social worker, and position the social worker as a hero in a variety of settings. A number of "turnaround" stories were also later developed into print ads.

Based on the target audience that was defined during the research process—Sandwich Generation Women—a strategic partnership was formed with *O, The Oprah Magazine*, one of the country's hottest media properties. A print and e-mail ad campaign was conducted in 2006 that featured four of these "turnaround" stories.

NASW regional chapters were inspired by the new campaign and began making requests to the national organization for general ads that they could place at the grassroots level. To meet this need, Crosby Marketing developed general message ads that demonstrate the depth and breadth of the social work profession. Each of these ads helped to explain the variety of job descriptions and settings in which social workers work. These ads were compiled into a chapter toolkit, which gave local chapters advice about how to use the advertisements and included various formats. The materials provided included billboards, transit ads, print ads, and small-space materials. Chapters have been very successful in placing these on the local level.

Utilizing a unique media venue, the campaign was taken to new heights with a billboard in Times Square during the 2005 holiday season (Next Page). The multimedia billboard reinforced messages from the general ads to explain the depth and breadth of ways that social workers help.

In the summer of 2006, Crosby worked with NASW and a social work partner, the New York Academy of Medicine, to conduct a survey among the campaign target audience about their experiences with aging parents. "Squeezed Between Children and Older Parents: A Survey of Sandwich Generation Women" was a national poll conducted among 1,000 women ages 35 to 54. The survey showed that although these women experience higher levels of stress and unhappiness than the general population, they have not sought help for their problems and often aren't aware of the resources available through the help of a social worker. The survey gave NASW an opportunity for even more publicity.

4. Evaluating Results

• The consumer website now contains more than 250 pages of information on 30 consumer-interest topics. By late 2006, the site had received more than 2 million hits, with an average of 70,000 hits per day.

• Four print ads appeared in *O, The Oprah Magazine* in September 2006, fueling a 260 percent increase in traffic to the website over previous months.

• All 56 NASW chapters adopted the "helping" profession position
and provided extensive grassroots exposure. They placed print,
outdoor, and transit advertising reaching more than 12 million
viewers throughout the country.

• Results of the survey among Sandwich Generation Women were
publicized with national media outlets and garnered coverage in
USA Today, United Press International, The CBS Early Show, and *Health
Magazine.*

The CORE process had successfully helped guide a major, national
integrated campaign.

Chapter 7

Don't Sell Rotten Fish

Sending the Right Message to the Customer

Two boys are playing hockey on a pond in Boston Common when one is attacked by a rabid Rottweiler. Thinking quickly, the other boy takes his stick, wedges it down the dog's collar and twists, breaking the dog's neck. A reporter who was strolling by sees the incident, and rushes over to interview the boy. "Young Bruins Fan Saves Friend From Vicious Animal," he starts writing in his notebook.

"But I'm not a Bruins fan," the little hero replied.

"Sorry. Since we're in Boston, I just assumed you were," said the reporter and starts again. "Red Sox Fan Rescues Friend From Horrific Attack" he writes in his notebook.

"I'm not a Red Sox fan either," says the boy.

"I always assume everyone in Boston is either for the Bruins or Red Sox. What team do you root for?" the reporter asked.

"I'm a Yankees fan," said the child.

The reporter starts a new sheet in his notebook and writes, "Little Bastard from New York Kills Beloved Family Pet."

This joke illustrates how people can send faulty messages because of their biases. Bias in your communications is one of several key barriers to sending consistent, meaningful messages. For example, how many people believe the car dealer who goes on TV claiming he is offering the best price and service in town, especially since four or five dealers do it at the same time, on the same channel?

A related barrier is the bane of the PR practitioner, i.e., exaggerating what you have to offer.

When I was a kid, local fishmongers would ride carts through residential neighborhoods, shouting "Fresh fish for sale." A great way to market fish—unless it wasn't really fresh. Selling old or spoiled fish was not only a way to lose that buyer, but the whole neighborhood would know it in a hurry.

Don't puff up your offering. If you promise more than you can deliver, your neighborhood of customers will catch on quickly, especially in these days of electronic connectivity among consumers. That doesn't mean you can't design your message to appeal more to the customer. I discovered the value of that on a trip to the Atlantis resort in the Bahamas. It is located on what used to be called "Hog Island," which was going nowhere as a tourist spot until they changed the name to "Paradise Island."

Positive messages are a way to cut through the media clutter, a cacophony of messages grown exponentially by Internet applications. It's increasingly difficult to be heard, much less understood in our over-communicated world. I harken back to integrated marketing communications as a way to help cut through the clutter.

Having all of your communications speak with one voice helps guarantee your message gets through to your target audience. Of course, noise by itself isn't enough. You must know who you're communicating with, what they want or need, and how to reach them emotionally.

Play on Their Emotions

In my newspaper days, I often noticed how an emotional story would move people to action. I saw such stories make people cry. (That's where we get the term "sob story," usually an account of personal troubles that is meant to arouse sympathy.) I've read and written articles that moved readers to join a cause or make a donation. I once wrote a sob story about a poor family's tragedy that left them penniless and, shortly after it appeared in the paper, I received a pile of mail in which I discovered cash and checks made out to me to give to the family. I realized then that the best way to move people to action was to play on their feelings. I discovered that sending messages could be related to the ancient maxim that people are motivated by both positive and negative emotions—such as love and kindness, fear and greed.

My intuitive discovery has been backed up by behavioral research. Behavioral scientists studying the brain have debunked the idea that decisions are made mostly through logical, linear thinking. They discovered that emotions are critical in retaining and retrieving messages. In a 2007 landmark study by a Task Force of the American Association of Advertising Agencies (AAAA) and Advertising Research Foundation (ARF), this finding was applied to marketing. The study determined that advertising messages that successfully generate a strong emotional reaction create better recall, persuasion, and liking than those that don't.

The traditional thought about how people responded to advertising messages was "Think, Feel, Act." But the AAAA/ARF researchers found that when viewing an ad, consumers follow a different path to a purchase decision—"First FEEL, Then Think, Then Act."

This idea makes sense when you consider that consumers are emotional beings with imaginations who create a loyal relationship in their minds with certain brands. As the Task Force study concludes: "As marketers, creatives, planners and researchers gain a clearer understanding of how story line, metaphor and emotion drive idea engagement, we are going to see a rise in the number of powerful, lasting advertising ideas which create brand demand and a lessening on any single platform. They will generate effectiveness by engagement, rather than by repetition or tonnage." In other words, while increased media spending and more media outlets help get the message out, it may not be effective if the message doesn't connect with customers.

A later (2009) study by the AAAAs confirmed these earlier findings, reporting that "Emotional advertising is more effective than rational appeals." This report explained what is meant by rational and emotional advertising appeals:

- "Rational or informational appeals focus on the consumer's practical, functional, or utilitarian need for a product or service. These ads lay out the reasons for purchase by emphasizing features and attributes of the brand and the benefits resulting from its use."

- "Emotional appeals relate to consumers' social or psychological needs. This messaging uses feelings, poignancy, humor, excitement and other engaging tactics to evoke emotional responses, thereby playing into people's desire for love, belonging, security, self-esteem, status, etc., and connecting those positive feelings with the brand. (Note that "emotional" is not synonymous with 'creative'—puppies and heartwarming family scenes are not necessarily creative, and many creative ads aren't particularly emotive.)"

The report concluded that emotional messaging creates an enduring sense of brand differentiation, reduces price sensitivity, and increases sales. For proof, the report cited an analysis of 880 winners of Advertising Effectiveness Awards from the United Kingdom's Institute of Practitioners in Advertising which, for example, revealed that:

- "Emotionally based campaigns outperformed rationally based campaigns on every single business measure in the cases studied—sales, market share, profit, penetration, loyalty and price sensitivity.

- "Emotional appeals are almost twice as likely to generate large profit gains as rational ones.

- "The more emotion dominates over rational messaging, the bigger the impact on the business; the most effective ads are those with little or no rational content.

- "Emotional advertising is particularly good at reducing price sensitivity, and hence leads to large profit gains.

- "Emotional campaigns create an enduring sense of differentiation for the brand.

- "Even in categories that are supposedly rational, like computers and financial services, people go with their gut feelings first.

- "Emotional engagement increases in importance during the product's life cycle, as persuasion-based strategies progressively decline in effectiveness.

- "The exception is direct response advertising, which seems to require a more rational approach."

The 2009 AAAAs report also gave examples of then current brands that "own" emotions:

- "Michelin's image of a baby playing in a tire, combined with the compelling message about how much is "riding on your tires," evokes guilt and the powerful motivation of protecting your family; New York Life does the same thing with its 'selfless gift' campaign.

- " 'Miller Time' evokes the positive feelings of relaxing after work with a shorthand slogan. People already know the product features, so this is a purely emotional trigger.

- "Starbucks, iPod, Hallmark, eBay, Blackberry, Nike, Viagra and Virgin satisfy emotional desires while avoiding reference to product features in their ads.

- "Corona beer's 'vacation in a bottle' imagery.

- "The Kleenex 'Let It Out' campaign has real people expressing emotions and links the brand to emotional catharsis.

- "Tide fights commoditization by aligning itself with the emotional relationship women have with their clothing, and recognizes how clothing plays into their lifestyle aspirations. By letting Tide take care of the laundry, women can focus on the important things.

- "MasterCard shows how a credit card can enrich consumers' lives with its very successful—and emotional—'Priceless' campaign."

Like its predecessor study with partner ARF, the study pointed out that customers make decisions emotionally, then justify them rationally.

Telling Stories

Another key conclusion of both studies is that the most effective way to produce emotion and engagement is through storytelling. As the AAAA/ARF report states, "we believe engaging in storytelling ads will also prove superior in creating connections with consumers that enrich brand meaning and ultimately impact brand behavior."

The Task Force explained how it works. The story the ad tells engages the consumer's emotions and triggers stored memories—association, stories, brand experiences and images—that produce emotional response.

"Memories have a deep association with storytelling," the study says. "To tell a story is to remember an important idea—we remember by telling stories—it is something we virtually have to do. As agents of the larger society, stories help consumers create memories and hence define their self-identities and interpret cultural trends and rituals. Companies use storytelling to shape the memories which consumers record and recall. Hence, the memory and meaning assigned by the consumer to a brand is one co-created by the advertiser and the consumer. Today, advertisers have to take a fresh look at their target prospects as human beings with emotions as well as thoughts, and stories as well as facts."

The Task Force study included a number of brand campaign examples of storytelling. I'll briefly recount two of them—Campbell's Soup and Southwest Airlines TV ad campaigns—that linked a strong emotional response (humor for Southwest and empathy for Campbell's) to storytelling.

The Campbell TV commercial is the story of a little girl being escorted to her new foster parents' home. The initial anxiety and sadness from her loss is turned into a soft smile when the foster mother brings the girl a bowl of Campbell's noodle soup. The commercial, called "Orphan," generated an 80 percent purchase interest with the majority rating the commercial believable. When compared to a competitor's commercial that focused on taste and quality ingredients, "Orphan" delivered much higher purchase intent through an emotional story.

The second example of emotional linkage was Southwest Airlines' commercial, "Want To Get Away," which portrayed a humorous, embarrassing moment (snooping into a friend's medicine chest out of curiosity only for it to crash into the sink). The commercial linked this story with the brand's offer to get away at an attractive low price. When compared to a competitor's commercial, the Southwest ad scored much higher on motivation and imagination.

True stories can have an equal emotional impact. In fact, true stories can be more interesting, more plausible, and more convincing. As noted in the NASW case history in Chapter VI, to demonstrate how social workers help, my agency used a number of real stories to link the audience to the association's brand. These stories, used in ads and on the

NASW website, detailed a "turnaround" or how lives were changed through the help of a social worker.

Here are two of the ads to show how storytelling worked in this campaign.

A SOCIAL WORKER HELPED HIM PUT THE WAR

6,800 MILES BEHIND HIM.

The social worker is Rick Selig, PhD, LSCSW, who counsels veterans in his private practice in Kansas. The soldier is Army National Guard Specialist Chuck Ross. They met when Chuck returned from his tour in Iraq. Finding himself hypersensitive and easily angered, Chuck knew he needed coping skills for being back home — where loud noises aren't attacks and lives aren't always on the line. Dr. Selig, a specialist in trauma and stress, helped Chuck practice coping techniques to "downshift" his reactions from high alert to everyday life. Four months later, he's been able to put the stress of war half a world away. For veterans, for families, help starts with a social worker. To find out more about these and other life issues or to find a social worker, visit HelpStartsHere.org.

Social Workers
Help starts here.

Sponsored by the National Association of Social Workers

A SOCIAL WORKER FOUND THE RIGHT WORDS
TO END HER SILENCE.

He reached out to her by speaking Korean. He is Byung Tae Choi, MSW, a bilingual social worker with St. Barnabas Senior Services in Los Angeles. And his help transforms the lives of people like Eun Joo Choi, a recent arrival in America. After an accident left her isolated and deeply depressed, Byung brought a world of resources to Mrs. Choi, from counseling and translation services, to social events like Korean-American feasts and even group dances. Breaking down the barriers has given Mrs. Choi a new purpose, and something more. Friends. For seniors, for people of all ages, help starts with a social worker. **Tell us your story, or find a social worker, at www.HelpStartsHere.org.**

Social Workers
Help starts here.

The AAAA/ARF researchers selected the term "engagement" to define consumer responses to marketing messages. "Engagement is about creating relationships between consumers and brands," they wrote. "We believe engaging storytelling ads will also prove superior in creating connections with consumers that enrich brand meaning and ultimately impact brand behavior."

The impact on behavior through storytelling ads is proven constantly. For instance, as I was writing this book, the police department in Gwent, Wales, produced a TV PSA telling the emotional story of two teen girls giggling over a text message they are sending while driving down a country road. Distracted, the driver smashes head-on into another car and is then hit by a third. The carnage, including several deaths, is shown realistically and the message is clear—texting while driving is terribly dangerous. Digital special effects were used to show the horrors of the story. In this case, fear would be the motivator for viewers and regulators.

In discussing the PSA with Today Show host Ann Curry, noted advertising executive Donny Deutsch praised the storytelling nature of the PSA. He told Curry that he believes viewers watching the story of a nice teen girl who ultimately kills four people could exponentially speed up the process for barring texting while driving. Deutsch told Curry that presenting hard facts about distracted drivers has limited impact compared to showing people the human toll of driving while texting. "You know what, Ann," he said to Curry, "you increase your risk 23 times when texting, and you go 'OK;' we hear the numbers, we hear of the fatalities, but you never actually see it this graphic. It's one thing to intellectually get it into our brains, but when you see it this graphically . . . I tell you, I couldn't get through this [ad]."

In the first few days of viewing, more than a million people watched the PSA on YouTube. I'm sure some of them did what I did, made sure my teenage grandchildren who drive knew about the PSA.

As a viewer as well as a writer, I personally have experienced the power of storytelling in changing behavior. Back in 1967, when my son, Raymond, was five years old and I was a 2-pack-a-day cigarette smoker who tried to quit many times, I happened to see a TV commercial that changed my life. It was a PSA from the American Heart Association titled "Like Father, Like Son." It depicted a father doing chores that his young four- or five-year-old copied. Then, they sit down at a tree together, the dad lights up a cigarette and drops the pack at his side, where the son is sitting. The little boy picks up the pack and starts to take out a cigarette. The announcer's final words were, "Like Father, Like Son—Think about it."

I thought about it and quit on the spot. Not that quitting was easy, but I never smoked again, and it gave me the ammunition later to stop my then teenage son from smoking—without my being a hypocrite.

For me, all the statistics about the evils of smoking, including the Surgeon General's report on smoking's disastrous results, which came out a few years earlier, were nowhere near as powerful as that one story about father and son.

So, when you want to get an emotional reaction from customers, don't use statistics, don't use adjectives, and don't pontificate. Tell them a story.

Although this kind of emotional engagement of the audience has been proven successful, its implementation is sporadic.

Traditional marketers have been functioning in the old "Think. Feel. Act." mode for so long, they have difficulty changing the emphasis to "Feel. Think. Act." It's not easy to produce genuine emotion. If customers feel they are being manipulated by the message, their reaction may be negative, and that negativity can be associated with the brand.

When marketing, you can't always tell stories, of course. Sometimes you must recount the features and benefits of your organization, its products or services. But remember, you're dealing with human beings, and relating your brand to their emotional attitudes and memories is the best way to impact their behavior.

Even features and benefits can often be wrapped up in an emotional story. For example, selling the dryness, fit, or protection of diapers can move mothers to a purchase decision more easily if you tell a compelling story showing babies in diapers.

To give a brand credibility and appeal, the promises represented by its messages must provide evidence that your offering is meaningful and valuable to the customer. Supporting emotional connection with genuine, credible value, which may include features and benefits, will move the customer more easily to your desired action.

One more caution. When sending your engaging message, your language must be clear. I'll use another joke to make the point:

A panda walks into a cafe. He orders a sandwich, eats it, then draws a gun and fires two shots in the air.

"Why?" asks the confused waiter, as the panda makes towards the exit. The panda produces a badly punctuated wildlife manual and tosses it over his shoulder.

"I'm a panda," he says, at the door. "Look it up."

The waiter turns to the relevant entry and, sure enough, finds an explanation.

"Panda. Large black-and-white bear-like mammal, native to China. Eats, shoots and leaves."

Even a tiny comma can cause confusion. The motivational power of language is timeless, and the poets of the past knew how to make an emotional connection with their audience. But marketers aren't Shakespeares, so it's a challenge to send emotional messages to customers. Understanding your customers' language is necessary for you to communicate effectively with them. Language, especially storytelling, allows you to connect with your customers. In the Internet age, it's more important than ever to know the words that express your customers' needs. If you want your customers to find you on search engines, you must use key words that they're looking for. There are untold numbers of books on writing, so I won't go into tips on communicating with emotion here. But even though I'm being redundant, there's one tip worth repeating: the most important step in communicating with your customers is knowing who they are, what they want or need, and how to reach them emotionally.

In other words, "Hear Thy Customers" before sending them messages. Just how to do that is part of the marketing research discussion of Chapter III, "Just Who Is Your Customer." That section suggested the best ways to find out what customers and prospects want—or what your audiences think of your organization, its products or services, and its messages.

We mentioned surveys, from the simple restaurant questionnaire to Wal-Mart's complex surveys reaching 500,000 to a million customers monthly to online, computerized questioning. They all have their place in the research mode. But there's no better way to "hear thy customers" than talking to them one-on-one. You and your staff can do that when you meet, greet, or serve them in your office or store or, more formally, using such techniques as street corner interviews or mall intercepts. The technique I have found most illuminating is the focus group.

Focus Groups

Focus groups are no substitute for quantitative audience research, which is used to develop actual numbers of audience members in order to accurately measure market situations. Qualitative research, on the other hand, tries to understand human behavior by investigating the why and how of decisions. The findings of qualitative research, including focus groups, cannot be projected to the population of your audience as a whole.

But in the relaxed atmosphere of a properly run focus group, your target audience usually will feel more comfortable in discussing their reactions, opinions, and ideas. Focus groups can provide guidance for developing and testing messages, screening new ideas or concepts, and understanding your audience's point of view.

Focus groups can also be valuable first steps in quantitative research, identifying key issues, or determining the language to use in a questionnaire or survey.

Properly conducting a focus group is critical and requires care in recruiting participants, finding a moderator, and choosing the right facility. If properly conducted, however, focus groups can provide you with invaluable customer feedback, especially in developing and testing messages for your customers.

The impact of focus groups on message development can be seen in the case history of the National Association of Social Workers (NASW) in Chapter VI.

"Help Starts Here"

Focus groups were part of the research used to help develop a branding strategy to change misperceptions of the social work profession. In eight focus groups, six among the general public and two among social workers, we used preliminary messages as a way of generating discussion on relevant topics. In the discussions, led by a professional moderator, the groups were presented more than a dozen preliminary creative concepts, taglines, and message statements for testing. While a number of them appealed to the participants, the concept with the most appeal used the headline "Social Workers Help People Help Themselves."

The analysis of the research led to the conclusion that the general public related best with helping people help themselves in diverse settings, and that social workers themselves related best with defining their profession as educated, experienced professionals who solve the problems of living. These conclusions led to development of NASW's new positioning statement:

> *"Social workers have the right education, experience and dedication to help people help themselves whenever and wherever they need it most."*

That positioning, in turn, was expressed in a campaign tagline, "Help Starts Here." We added a helping hand logo, and you saw the result in the preceding chapter:

Social Workers
Help starts here.

Thus, listening to the customers—in this case the public and social workers themselves—led to an effective brand identity that could be communicated through emotional stories of helping people. It all came together through integrated marketing communications.

CHAPTER 8

AIDA—Marketing's Selfish Princess

Models for Delivering Creative Messages

Discussing the delivery of emotional messages, as we did in the previous chapter, reminds me of a chat I had recently with my friend and mentor Os Guinness, noted social critic and author of more than 20 books.

Around the time I started writing this book, Os and I were chatting over dinner about ideas for his latest manuscript, including a concept he calls "creative persuasion." It's the challenge of making people see something that is not readily apparent. The challenge, as Os put it, "is to trigger a shift in thinking through a question, a story, or a drama that, through a punch line, reveals a whole new way of seeing things." There are dramatic messages, Os explained, that not only get an audience's attention but persuade people to act differently than they would normally.

The proverbial light bulb went on for me as we discussed his concept. As I explained to Os, it reminded me of AIDA, the traditional acronym for an ideal advertising message that also seeks "creative persuasion":

$\underline{\textbf{A}}$ = Get Attention
$\underline{\textbf{I}}$ = Arouse Interest
$\underline{\textbf{D}}$ = Stimulate Desire
$\underline{\textbf{A}}$ = Obtain Action

While emotional stories can drive behavior through a "Feel, Think, Act" path, the scientific practice of marketing has produced various models to help move people to action, and AIDA is one of the oldest.

Developed in the 1930s, the AIDA model helps map how messages move customers from attraction to action. The formula is ubiquitous in marketing, whether you're creating an ad, designing a brochure, writing a news release, building a website, etc.

A = If you don't attract the customer's attention, all else will fail. The attention getting elements of the communication—the headline or title, the graphic, the sound, the person or place involved—must resonate with the reader/viewer/visitor.

I = What does your communication offer to benefit customers, solve their problems, allay their fears, foster their altruism? By demonstrating these benefits or advantages, you will arouse their interest.

D = To stimulate desire, connect the benefits to the customers' wants and needs. What do the customers get if they take advantage of your offering? How will it satisfy them? Stimulating desire is easier said than done. That's why you must make sure the customers know specifically "What's in it for me?" —and make them believe they must have your product or service or act on your idea. Let them know what they will miss if they don't get your offering.

A = Once you have engaged the customers, tell them what to do. It's similar to fund-raising. All the lead up is worthless if you don't "make the ask." Send them to your store, the website, the blog, the phone, the mailbox, or the fax machine to purchase, to seek information, to join or inquire.

There is no guarantee that AIDA or any other model will get your message through to the customer. Even with emotional stories, the customer may not always understand or accept your message. But if you know your customers' needs, emotions, and interests, AIDA can help you communicate accurately and successfully.

AIDA In Action

You can see AIDA in action in earlier ads in this book, e.g., the National Association of Social Workers "story" ads and the "Like Father, Like Son" TV PSA that helped me kick the smoking habit. But I'd like to use another ad, produced by my agency, that clearly demonstrates the AIDA model. The ad appears below with a graphic and headline that grabs your attention.

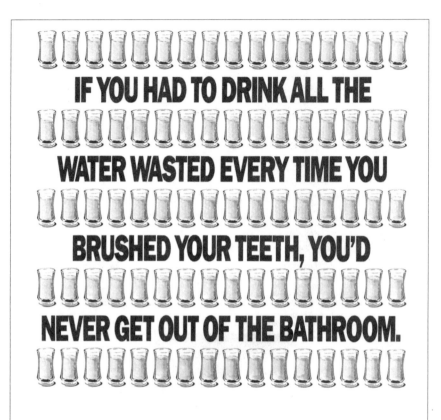

IF YOU HAD TO DRINK ALL THE WATER WASTED EVERY TIME YOU BRUSHED YOUR TEETH, YOU'D NEVER GET OUT OF THE BATHROOM.

If you leave the faucet on when you brush your teeth, up to five gallons of water – 80 glasses – go down the drain with your toothpaste.

Just by turning off the water while you brush, you'll help preserve a scenic river. You'll help reduce the cost of water and sewage treatment. And you'll lower your water bill.

So the next time you brush, please don't use so much water. Unless of course, you're very thirsty.

Your donation will establish scholarships for environmental education. Send your contribution to: The Environmental Challenge Fund, Radio City Station, P.O. Box 1138, New York, NY 10101-1138.

This advertisement was prepared for the TIME Environmental Challenge as a public service by Crosby Communications, Inc.

Eighty glasses of water depicted in rows interspersed with the headline, "If you had to drink all the water wasted every time you brush your teeth, you'd never get out of the bathroom" certainly grabs your attention, even begins to arouse your interest. That interest is heightened when the first line of copy explains that if you leave on the faucet when you brush your teeth, you waste five gallons—80 glasses of water. So what's the desire aroused? The copy goes on to explain that by turning off the water you'll benefit in many ways—preserve a scenic river, reduce the cost of water and sewage treatment, and lower your water bill. The call to action: when you brush, turn off the faucet.

How much action did the ad produce? I can't tell you, specifically. But I can tell you that the ad was one of only 10 "most powerful" winners from among 325 ads submitted by agencies to *Time* magazine's 1990 Environmental Challenge. The ad not only appeared in *Time* but, through my agency's publicity, in most of our local papers. Better yet, to this day, I still have people in social settings tell me, "I turn off the water when I'm brushing my teeth because of your glasses ad." Now that's "creative persuasion."

I'm doubly proud of that ad, first, because it won the *Time* challenge and, second, because the art director who designed it was Belinda Crosby Butler, my daughter, who worked for Crosby Marketing at the time. Oh, by the way, I always turn off the faucet when I brush my teeth.

Advertising's Selfish Princess

You might be asking why I call AIDA "Advertising's Selfish Princess." If you're musically inclined, you'll recognize Aida as an Italian grand opera by Verdi and the name of its heroine, the Princess Aida. To me, AIDA is marketing royalty that only works if she answers a customer's selfish question: "What's in it for me?" Often called by its initials, WIIFM defines the purpose of the message: satisfying the customer. In fact, some marketers have taken the formula one step further in its evolution, adding an "S" for customer Satisfaction, making the model AIDAS. The added value of following the AIDA model is keeping your messages selfishly centered on the customer and not on the organization, its products or services.

Admittedly, some marketers believe AIDA's time has passed. These detractors call AIDA too simplistic, too hierarchical, or too tied to traditional linear thoughts. In fact, the AAAA/ARF Task Force study related AIDA to the outmoded "Think-Feel-Do" mental model of how advertising works. The study said, "the old AIDA mental model" is "incorrect since the underlying assumptions that consumers take decisions in a linear way and behavior is guided by rational-only principles do not hold in the light of the new knowledge about the human brain."

Since I subscribe to the value of emotional story-telling, how can I disagree with the Task Force? As you undoubtedly are aware by now, while I revere many marketing gurus, I don't always agree with them. For example, my definition of "customer" is a bit outside the standard box. Another example: I believe Professor Philip Kotler's definition of "brand" is more a definition of brand identity. Well, the same is true of the AAAA/ARF opinion of AIDA. Where I disagree is in the Task Force's definition of AIDA as a "mental model." I don't look at it that way. To me, AIDA is not a "mental model" but a "message model," a road map for creating communications that connect with the customer. It is the message that gets attention, arouses interest, stimulates desire, and obtains action. There's no reason AIDA can't conform to "Feel-Think-Do." Grabbing attention can be done emotionally and arousing interest and creating desire can be achieved through storytelling.

AIDA's still a marketing princess in my book. In fact, rather than thinking her time has passed, I believe AIDA is a time-tested model, even more important in the new online, interactive world with its growing numbers of media and messages seeking your time and attention. AIDA can help get your messages heard amidst all the noise.

Message Models by Kiplinger and Stone

There are many communications models besides AIDA; one especially that has helped me as a marketer from the beginning—because I learned it in my last salaried job as a journalist. (I say "salaried" because I published tourist magazines for 20 years as part of my agency.)

That job was with the Kiplinger organization in Washington, D.C., and the lesson I learned there was how to deliver direct response messages. I was Associate Editor of Kiplinger's *Changing Times* magazine, and it fascinated me back then that the magazine and the well-known Kiplinger newsletters succeeded on subscriptions—no advertising. Founded in 1947, *Changing Times* didn't begin carrying advertising until 1980. It changed its name to *Kiplinger's Personal Finance* magazine in 1991 and continues to prosper.

Besides pioneering the newsletter format and personal finance coverage, Kiplinger was an early adopter of new methods for selling subscriptions. It perfected direct mail, radio, and television direct response techniques. For example, in 1952, when NBC launched "The Today Show," advertising was hard to come by. NBC couldn't land one advertiser until Kiplinger bought commercials for *Changing Times* and drew a strong viewer response with direct response selling techniques that paralleled the AIDA model—especially because they used a glib pitch man and a sample issue offer to arouse interest and incite action. You can see the parallel especially in Kiplinger's direct mail letter, one of the most famous in marketing history. (See Exhibit A). With minor changes, the letter beat all tests against it for more than 40 years. It was so successful that the late Bob Stone, direct mail pioneer and marketer extraordinaire, used it as the classic example of his seven-step formula for what he called "Champion" letters.

Stone, in his famous book *Successful Direct Marketing Methods*, still in publication, extolled the direct mail letter generally for its capacity for "personal, one-on-one communication."

While his formula is for sales letters, it is relevant to any marketing communication. When reading the formula below, you will experience echoes of AIDA. Stone says make your most important point first—which translates to "Grab attention." The formula suggests "Arousing Interest" by enlarging on your most important benefit and telling the reader what's in it for him or her. By not only discussing what you are going to get but also what you might lose if you don't act, the formula "Stimulates Desire." And, finally, it says, "Incite Action. Now."

Here's Bob Stone's formula as he wrote it in *Successful Direct Marketing Methods*:

The Seven-Step Formula For Champion Letters
If any one piece in a direct mail package is key, that piece is the letter. One of the prime advantages of direct mail is its capacity for personal, one-on-one communication, and the letter provides that personal communication. It's no wonder, then, that more has been written about how to create a good direct mail letter than about any other part of the direct mail package.

Here's a letter-writing formula that has served me well. I believe it follows a more detailed route than most formulas. And, used wisely, it should not stifle your creativity.

1. Promise your most important benefit in your headline or first paragraph. You simply can't go wrong by leading off with the most important benefit to the reader. Some writers believe in the slow buildup. But most experienced writers favor making the important point first. Many writers use the "Johnson Box": short, terse copy that summarizes the main benefits, positioned in a box above the salutation.

2. Immediately enlarge on your most important benefit. This step is crucial. Many writers come up with a great lead, then fail to follow through. Or they catch attention with their heading, but then take two or three paragraphs to warm up to their subject. The reader's attention is gone! Try hard to elaborate on your most important benefit right away, and you'll build up interest fast.

3. Tell readers specifically what they are going to get. It's amazing how many letters lack details on such basic product features as size, color, weight, and sales terms. Perhaps the writer is so close to the proposition that he or she assumes the readers know all about it. A dangerous assumption! And when you tell the reader what they are going to get, don't overlook the intangibles that go along with your product or service. For example, they are getting smart appearance in addition to a pair of slacks, knowledge in addition to a 340-page book.

4. Back up your statements with proof and endorsements. Most prospects are somewhat skeptical about advertising. They know it sometimes gets a little overenthusiastic about a product. So they accept it with a grain of salt. If you can back up your own statements with third-party testimonials or a list of satisfied users, everything you say becomes more believable.

5. Tell readers what they might lose if they don't act. As noted, people respond affirmatively either to gain something they do not possess or to avoid losing something they already have. Here's a good spot in your letter to overcome human inertia—imply what could be lost if action is postponed. People don't like to be left out. A skillful writer can use this human trait as a powerful influence in his or her message.

6. Rephrase your prominent benefits in your closing offer. As a good salesperson does, sum up the benefits to the prospect in your closing offer. This is the proper prelude to asking for action. This is where you can intensify the prospect's desire to have the product. The stronger the benefits you can persuade the reader to recall, the easier it will be for him or her to justify an affirmative decision.

7. Incite action. Now. This is the spot where you win or lose the battle with inertia. Experienced advertisers know that once a letter is put aside or tossed into a file, they're out of luck. So wind up with a call for action and a logical reason for acting now. Too many letters close with a statement like "supplies are limited." That argument lacks credibility. Today's consumer knows you probably have a warehouse full of merchandise. So make your reason a believable one. For example, "It could be many months before we go back to press on this book." Or "Orders are shipped on a first-come basis. The sooner yours is received, the sooner you can be enjoying your new widget."

In *Successful Direct Marketing Methods*, Stone reprinted the famous Kiplinger letter. Notice how closely the letter's structure resembles Bob Stone's formula. Though historically dated, its basic tenets are still true. Here's a reproduction of the letter, with indications of the formula in the right margin:

STANLEY R. MAYES *ASSISTANT TO THE PRESIDENT*

THE KIPLINGER WASHINGTON EDITORS, INC.

1729 H STREET, NORTHWEST, WASHINGTON, D.C. 20006   TELEPHONE: 887-6400

THE KIPLINGER WASHINGTON LETTER   THE KIPLINGER TAX LETTER
THE KIPLINGER AGRICULTURAL LETTER   THE KIPLINGER FLORIDA LETTER
THE KIPLINGER CALIFORNIA LETTER   THE KIPLINGER TEXAS LETTER
CHANGING TIMES MAGAZINE

More Growth and Inflation Ahead...
and what YOU can do about it.

> 1. Most prominent benefit

   The next few years will see business climb to the highest
level this country has ever known. And with it...inflation.

   This combination may be hard for you to accept under today's
conditions. But the fact remains that those who do prepare for both
inflation AND growth ahead will reap big dividends for their foresight,
and avoid the blunders others will make.

> 2. Enlarging upon benefit

   You'll get the information you need for this type
of planning in the Kiplinger Washington Letter...
and the enclosed form will bring you the next 26
issues of this helpful service on a "Try-out" basis.
The fee: Less than 81¢ per week...only $21 for the
6 months just ahead...and tax deductible for business
or investment purposes.

> 3. Telling reader specifically what he is going to get

   During the depression, in 1935, the Kiplinger Letter warned
of inflation and told what to do about it. Those who heeded its advice
were ready when prices began to rise.

   Again, in January of 1946, the Letter renounced the widely-
held view that a severe post-war depression was inevitable. Instead
it predicted shortages, rising wages and prices, a high level of
business. And again, those who heeded its advice were able to avoid
losses, to cash in on the surging economy of the late '40s, early '50s
and mid '60s. It then kept its clients prepared for the swings of the
'70s, keeping them a step ahead each time.

> 4. Proving the value with past experience

   Now Kiplinger not only foresees expansion ahead, but also
continuing inflation, and in his weekly Letter to clients he points
out profit opportunities in the future...and also dangers.

> 5. Tell the prospect what he will lose if he doesn't act

   The Kiplinger Letter not only keeps you informed of present
trends and developments, but also gives you advance notice on the
short & long-range business outlook...inflation forecasts...energy
predictions...housing...federal legislative prospects...politics...
investment trends & pointers...tax outlook & advice...labor, wage
settlement prospects...upcoming gov't rules & regulations.. ANYTHING
that will have an effect on you, your business, your personal finances,
your family.

> 6. Summarizing prominent benefits in closing offer

   To take advantage of this opportunity to try the Letter and
benefit from its keen judgments and helpful advice during the fast-

> 7. Inciting action NOW

                              (Over, please)

Exhibit A

<table>
<tr><td>7. Inciting
action NOW</td><td>changing months ahead...fill in and return the enclosed form along with your $21 payment. And do it with this guarantee: That you may cancel the service and get a prompt refund of the unused part of your payment any time you feel it is not worth far more to you than it costs.</td></tr>
</table>

changing months ahead...fill in and return the enclosed form along with your $21 payment. And do it with this guarantee: That you may cancel the service and get a prompt refund of the unused part of your payment any time you feel it is not worth far more to you than it costs.

I'll start your service as soon as I hear from you, and you'll have each weekly issue on your desk every Monday morning thereafter.

Sincerely,

Stanley Mayes
Assistant to the President

SAM:kga

P. S. More than half of all new subscribers sign up for a full year at $42. In appreciation, we'll send you FREE five special Kiplinger Reports on receipt of your payment when you take a full year's service, too. Details are spelled out on the enclosed slip. Same money-back guarantee and tax deductibility apply.

Seven-step formula and letter from **Successful Direct Marketing Methods,** *by Bob Stone. Sixth Edition. Copyright 1997 by NTC Business Books. Reprinted with permission of the McGraw-Hill Companies.*

In extolling the direct mail letter for its one-on-one communication, Bob Stone put his finger on the eternal marketing truth; no matter how it's done, in what media, to whatever audience, personalized communication is the most effective marketing method. Whether it is an age-old in-store promotion, or the traditional direct response vehicle, or the latest social media marketing, there's no substitute for being one-on-one with the customer.

CHAPTER 9

Avoiding the Myths of Marketing

Or, The Customer Isn't Always Right!

There are a multitude of business dos and don'ts that writers call "marketing myths." These notions vary from the old-time myths ("All publicity is good publicity") to new age fictions ("The Internet has killed traditional media").

While some of these myths are worth discussing, I'm most concerned about the unfounded concepts affecting your relationships with your customers. Until I went into business for myself, I was among the many who mouthed the bromide, "The customer is always right." It wasn't until I had customers of my own that I realized, while the customer is king, there is no divine right in that royalty.

The origin of the slogan "The customer is always right" goes back at least to 1908 when famous French hotelier César Ritz decreed, *"Le client n'a jamais tort,"* meaning the customer is never wrong. However, the "always right" version is credited first to American Harry Gordon Selfridge, founder of London's eponymous department stores. In the U.S. the slogan was most associated with Marshall Fields' department store in Chicago in the early 20th century. The idea was not to be taken literally, but as a way to show that these retailers put their customers first—to act as if the customers were right, even when they weren't.

Putting the customer first is a worthy policy, but it can have dangerous results in some cases. After eight chapters of telling you the value of king customer's loyalty and satisfaction, what can I say about dealing with customers' acts of disloyalty and dissatisfaction?

What I've learned over the years is that customers' wrongful or mis-guided acts require extraordinary action if you want to help your business, your employees, and your sanity. If you carry "The customer is always right" concept too far, it can come back to bite you. Once again, a joke helps make the point:

> *Department store manager* (chiding clerk): "What do you mean by arguing with that lady? Remember, the customer is always right!"

> *Clerk:* "But she said we were swindlers!"

Here are some lessons I've learned about dealing with misguided, even malevolent, customers.

Firing Your Customers

Sometimes, you have to fire a customer. Some customers can be bad for business. Abrasive, unreasonable, or abusive customers demand whatever they want because they believe "The customer is always right," and they can get away with it. It takes strong management to deal with these types. It's tough to give up a customer, especially when it's a major client or very profitable purchaser.

It didn't bother Herb Kelleher. Kelleher is the co-founder and for-mer chairman and CEO of Southwest Airlines. *Fortune* magazine called him perhaps the best CEO in America and named Southwest among the top five most admired corporations in the U.S. One of the reasons for both kudos is Southwest's and Kelleher's emphasis on customer service. But Kelleher's idea of customer service always came with a caveat—the customer is not always right. The classic example of firing a customer involves Herb Kelleher. As recounted in *Nuts: Southwest Airlines' Crazy Recipe for Business and Personal Success*, authors Kevin and Jackie Freiberg tell the story of a woman who always flew Southwest but was disappointed with every aspect of the airlines' operation. In fact, she became known as "Pen Pal" because after every flight she wrote in with a complaint. The Freibergs wrote about her:

> *"She didn't like the fact that the company didn't assign seats; she didn't like the absence of a first-class section; she didn't like not having a meal in flight; she didn't like Southwest's boarding procedure; she didn't like the color of the planes; she didn't like the flight attendants' sporty uni-*

forms and the casual atmosphere. And she hated peanuts! Her last let-
ter, reciting a litany of complaints, momentarily stumped Southwest's
customer relations people."

Since Southwest prides itself on answering every customer letter, explaining how it does things, the correspondence with "Pen Pal" was getting voluminous, until the matter was bumped up to Herb Kelleher's desk, with a note: "This one's yours." In sixty seconds, the story goes, Kelleher wrote back: "Dear Mrs. Crabapple, we will miss you. Love, Herb."

The Freibergs also recount Herb Kelleher's response to "Aren't the customers always right?

"No, they are not," Kelleher is reported responding. "And I think that's one of the biggest betrayals of employees a boss can possibly commit. The customer is sometimes wrong. We don't carry those sorts of customers. We write to them and say, 'Fly somebody else. Don't abuse our people.'"

Firing a customer is not always that easy, especially if it is long-standing and profitable. I have experienced that difficult choice several times.

For example, when one of our oldest and largest nonprofit clients brought in a new marketing director, I began hearing stories from my account representatives of chastisements from the new woman that bordered on verbal abuse. So, I scheduled a meeting with her to discuss the successful marketing partnership we had with her employer for a dozen years. At the meeting, when she began telling me how our relationship was going to be as a "vendor" not a marketing partner, I got a taste of what my account reps had experienced. But, "It's an old and valued client," I told myself, "Let's see if we can work to build a good relationship like the one we had with this client in the past." After all, we were the client's "agency of record." We had donated thousands of unpaid hours to this client and made cash contributions of more than $150,000 to its causes. I figured our loyalty ultimately would be rewarded. When the new marketing director decided to give some of our usual work to a competitor she claimed would do it "cheaper," that was the last straw. I felt the client was returning loyalty with disloyalty. That lack of loyalty broke the relationship and, even though she promised to let us "bid" on other jobs, I severed the relationship with a letter resigning from the account. To me, loyalty is a two-way street. So is respect between customer and seller and the seller's employees.

The Freibergs call their chapter discussing firing customers "Customers Come Second," meaning employees, not customers, come first. That's going a bit far, but in a strange way, putting your employees "first" actually results in putting your customers first—a classic example of a win-win situation. When you consider your employees to be number one, they tend to put your customers first. As I mentioned earlier, you should treat your employees as unique customers. They fit my definition of customers being "Those whose satisfaction is key to the organization's success."

As the Freibergs point out, "When employees feel they are treated humanely, when they receive 'legendary service,' they provide the kind of customer service for which Southwest Airlines is so well known."

Over the years, I have witnessed supervisors siding with unreasonable customers over employees. It's a very bad idea that results in worse customer service. If employees don't feel valued, they won't value customers.

Alternative Dispute Resolution

I don't want to give the impression that firing complaining or unreasonable customers is your best or only alternative. It should be a last resort, not an early response. Even Southwest suffered through voluminous correspondence with "Pen Pal" before Herb Kelleher told her goodbye. There are alternative ways to resolve disputes with customers.

I learned how important this is from a customer—DuPont Company's legal department. Often faced with legal battles with customers, suppliers, contractors, and joint venture partners, DuPont found that solving these battles with litigation was not only expensive and time-consuming, but negatively impacted some important business relationships.

So, DuPont Legal decided to emphasize Alternative Dispute Resolution (ADR) over litigation. ADR involves the use of mediation in appropriate cases and, at a higher level, arbitration, a more complex process based on contractual agreements. My client and friend Thomas L. Sager, General Counsel of DuPont, told me, "ADR can often lead to the resolution of conflicts in a way that meets our business needs while minimizing legal costs and business relationship issues."

I'm not suggesting that the average business would use such a legal process as ADR to resolve conflicts with customers. But the lesson of ADR is a simple one—when it comes to customers, try to make peace not war.

Given my preference for customer peacemaking over terminating, what is the ultimate conclusion about the myth? I'd say that while customers' wrongful or misguided acts shouldn't be excused with the "always right" presumption, such acts require the intelligent handling of your customers.

More Myths

Let me take this opportunity to clear up a few other confounding notions about marketing. This book has espoused certain marketing concepts and processes that have some mythology about them that you should understand.

The Planning Myth: In Chapter VI, I discussed the value of my agency's best practice, the marketing process. Some aspects of the marketing process can be given more credence than they deserve. The value of planning, for instance, is overrated if your objective is a marketing plan. I've written a few marketing plans for clients that never got off the shelf. The plan itself, no matter how good the research and thought behind it, is no good if it's not implemented.

I love *Selling The Invisible* author Harry Beckwith's example of the limitations of planning: "Don't assume that putting eight smart people in a room with good data will automatically produce something. Ford put eight smart planners in a room, and out popped the Edsel." (A "bit" oversimplified, as we'll explain when discussing the Edsel as a marketing mistake in Chapter XII.)

The Loyalty Myth: We've embraced the idea of obtaining customers and building their loyalty so you can profit from them over a lifetime. The danger in that concept is the impermanency of loyalty. Once you have a customer your relationship must be continually massaged to retain that loyalty. If you stand pat in the relationship, that customer may fade away. Remember, loyalty can erode through diminished service, reduced quality, or increased competition. Things can change quickly so you must always be on the lookout for evolving customer wants and needs and how to satisfy them.

The Product Myth: A myth that has been propagated over the years is that "A great product will sell itself." Not very likely. As explained in Chapter V, to build a successful brand you need all three legs of the brand-building stool—a quality product, supported by meaningful, consistent communications, and nurturing customer relations. In other words, even great products and services won't "sell" if the customer doesn't know about them and their benefits.

The "No Such Thing As Bad Publicity" Myth: Irish author Brendan Behan once said, "There is no such thing as bad publicity except your own obituary." In fact, scientific research has given some credibility to the idea that all publicity is good publicity. The scientists call it "attribute forgetting": The inability to remember specific characteristics of a person or event.

"Attribute forgetting" was confirmed through experiments by Kent University psychologist David Riccio, Ph.D., as he reported in *Psychology Today*: "Attributes disappear from our memory at different rates, but familiarity—the sense we've previously encountered a particular person, place or thing—tends to outlast other characteristics. Experiments show that people think more favorably of things they've seen before, even if they've forgotten having seen them. Come election day, we may vote for a politician because we remember his name—but not his recent indictment."

That may be true, but experience tells me the notion that all publicity is good publicity is dangerous. Bad publicity can severely damage an organization. Like selling rotten fish, bad news can travel fast in your customer neighborhood.

Back in my restaurant marketing days, I saw how bad local publicity—a poor newspaper critic's review or a failed health department inspection reported in the press—could reduce business significantly. If you don't respond properly to bad publicity it can do considerable damage to your reputation. You may remember these cases:

• In the 1990s, class action suits claiming that Dow Corning's silicone breast implants caused health problems resulted in a multi-billion dollar settlement that put Dow Corning in bankruptcy protection for nine years, ending in June 2004, and dented its reputation.

• The 1989 Exxon Valdez oil spill in Alaska caused wide criticism of Exxon for its slow response to cleaning up the disaster. Exxon responded to the criticism with a massive cleanup effort, but it cost Exxon billions of dollars in damages and untold reputation damages that are still being repaired more than 20 years later.

• When officials in North Carolina discovered the chemical benzene in bottles of Perrier mineral water in 1990, the company's reputation for purity suffered a blow. In responding to the crisis, Perrier shifted from explanation to explanation on the issue—a poor response. Finally, it recalled 160 million bottles of its water. It took several years for Perrier to repair its damaged reputation.

• Even when it's not your fault, a crisis can be damaging, as in the case of Johnson & Johnson's Tylenol. When an individual laced Tylenol with cyanide, killing seven people, the bad publicity caused the company's market value to drop by a billion dollars. However, Johnson & Johnson's quick and appropriate crisis management, including openness and development of a tamperproof package, saved the company's reputation and ultimately succeeded in preserving the long-term value of the brand.

A lesson I learned when I was a boy scout— "Be Prepared" —is applicable here. You must try to manage issues before they turn into crises and be ready if a crisis occurs.

Quite often image problems are caused by improper or knee-jerk responses to issues as they arise. Without a plan or process for managing such issues, they often become controversies or, worse yet, crises.

To negate this problem, organizations should undertake "issues management," which means anticipating and identifying issues and attempting to resolve them before they reach crisis levels. By managing your response, issues can be kept from erupting into crises and, if a crisis does ensue, its adverse effects can be minimized. An "issue" is defined as a matter in dispute. For example, a patient doesn't like a particular hospital's treatment and begins to talk about this dislike. These activities, either directly or indirectly, generate media attention. And media attention can turn an issue into a crisis.

To deal with issues management, you must first establish a permanent issues management team, which could consist of key staff members and/or outside advisors, such as your attorney. The team would be tasked to work out details of an issues management plan, which should include:

- An early warning system—a method for monitoring issues before they become crises.

- A list of the constituencies affected by the issues.

- Ready reference documents—media lists, etc. —and a physical issues management plan manual or internal Internet site.

- Who on the team will do what? Who is spokesperson? Who will prepare releases? Who will field phone calls?

- What constitutes an issue or crisis that requires assembling the team other than for regular meetings.

With such a team in place, you'll be prepared.

In Chapter IV, we discussed tips for good media relations. They'll come in handy in avoiding or coping with bad publicity.

The "End Of Advertising" Myth: The combination of the growth of online marketing and the decline of print media has some prognosticators predicting the demise of traditional marketing. Certainly online advertising, websites, social media, and search engines have added sharp, new arrows to the marketing quiver, but if you want to hit the target customer most effectively, you need to integrate these interactive methods with traditional techniques. For example, outdoor advertising, mainly billboards, are the second largest growth media behind online. Direct mail still works well in targeting specific markets, especially ones you have difficulty reaching online. TV, especially locally targeted ads on cable, is a great way to tell your story. And many print media, particularly small town local newspapers and national specialty magazines, are still viable.

Shooting down this myth is prologue to coming chapters, in which we discuss the new media and combining it with old media to broaden the reach of all media, from one channel to another, from person to person.

CHAPTER 10

The Internet Turns Marketing Topsy-Turvy

---◁◇▷---

Customer Engagement Differs in the Digital Age

The online marketing world is changing and growing as you read this. As I struggled with how to present the many facets of online marketing in the midst of warp speed change, I was reminded of my last journalistic employer, *Kiplinger's Changing Times* magazine, and the motto it carried in each issue, words from Ralph Waldo Emerson:

> *"This time, like all times, is a very good one, if we but know what to do with it."*

Online marketing has unbelievable potential if you "know what to do with it." I hope to shed some light on what to do with it in this and the next chapter. Even though the online world constantly changes, there are marketing opportunities available each time it changes, as the evolution of Web 1.0 to Web 2.0 so aptly attests. The opportunities are defined by the size of the audience. The heaviest Internet users spend one-third of their waking hours online. By 2013, the number of e-mail marketing messages sent annually is predicted to exceed 800 billion. (So as not to assume every reader is familiar with the many online applications, there's a glossary of key online terms at the end of this chapter.)

To see just how complex this online world is, you only have to view the various "Digital Ecosystem" charts displayed online. the one that follows, found on ecodigitalmarketing.com, is a good example. The Internet is an awesome marketing communications vehicle.

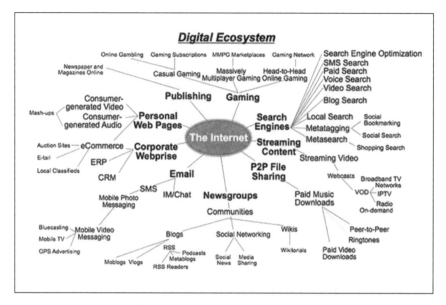

Reprinted courtesy of www.ecodigitalmarketing.com.

Before exploring the opportunities in this changing Internet landscape, I want to eliminate confusing terminology. Like the many synonyms for "customer," this new marketing has many names and facets, e.g., new media; online marketing; Internet marketing; e-commerce; interactive communications; electronic or e-marketing; the digital marketplace. While all of them will appear, as a catchall phrase, I'll use "online marketing."

Revolutionizing Communications

When the electronic computer was developed, the purpose was all about revolutionizing calculations. At first, the computer creators didn't realize that they were revolutionizing communications as well. As with any new communications vehicle, the marketers followed quickly on the heels of development. It was as true with the postal system, the telephone, radio, and television as it was with the computer.

Perhaps one of the most useful marketing devices of the last 25 years has been e-mail, short for electronic mail. E-mail began in the 1960s when many big companies operating mainframe and mini computers began using the e-mail facilities on those systems. Via terminals attached to these systems, even at remote branch offices, employees could send e-mails to each other. By the 1980s, the growth of the personal computer abetted the creation of a bunch of e-mail technologies.

Today, with the advent of the Internet, e-mail services are available to everyone who has a computer via web interfaces, usually without charge.

Enter the marketers. They quickly saw unfettered e-mail as an extension of direct mail marketing, only faster to the target audience and more interactive. I should say "we marketers" saw promotional value of e-mail. For years, at Crosby Marketing, we have used e-mail blasts successfully for clients for direct sales, fund-raising, information, education, and research.

The one-to-one e-mail is an easy way to contact a customer since almost everyone has e-mail, and it's so easy to use. But the e-mail blast, which allows you to reach multiple customers all at once, is an even more powerful tool.

Of course, as with any direct marketing, the list of recipients is the most important element. If you don't send your message to the right customer, it's a waste of time and money. You can purchase targeted e-mail lists from mailing list brokers. These lists usually are made up of people who have consented to receive services or information. The best list, I believe, is the one you build yourself by getting permission from your customers or contacts to communicate by e-mail. And your computer does much of the database building for you, recording the e-mail addresses of those who e-mail you.

Getting permission from your audience is called "permission marketing" or "opt-in e-mail." Thus when you use e-mail for marketing, say by sending a newsletter or product information, you give the recipient the chance to opt-in or opt-out of receiving similar, future e-mails. Once you get a contact to consent, you have qualified your list and have the greater ability to build a relationship or make a sale. It also means you won't become "SPAM" for the opt-in audience.

SPAM, or unsolicited e-mails, is the great bane of e-mail marketing. Not only does it clog your e-mail box, but it's confusing, sometimes disturbing, and occasionally it contains viruses that can shut down the organization's Internet service.

SPAM filters are essential for an organization receiving e-mail, but these filters won't protect the organization from the sheer volume of SPAM. Also, legitimate e-mails sometimes get filtered out with the SPAM. SPAM, and the increasing volume of e-mail, has alienated some consumers to e-mail marketing. Despite such negative feelings, e-mail promotions continue to generate strong response. Research indicates that almost half of Internet users say they are very or somewhat likely to take additional action after receiving an e-mail marketing message.

In the long run, for the marketer, the benefits of e-mail outweigh the negatives. Besides being pervasive and easy to use, e-mail marketing provides the following benefits:

- It's inexpensive, allowing you to distribute information to a broad audience at a relatively low cost.

- The back and forth potential of e-mail can improve one-to-one relationships with customers, the essence of brand-building.

- You can market anywhere because e-mail works worldwide.

- Delivery time is short, measured in seconds or minutes.

- E-mail results can be tracked easily through a number of tracking devices available both free and for a fee.

- E-mail users check their mail boxes constantly, ensuring your message gets through.

- You can rapidly conduct and tabulate audience surveys, using e-mail questionnaires.

- It allows you to distribute time-sensitive information, e.g., about new products or sales promotions.

- You can distribute key information to a variety of audiences— employees, stockholders, reporters, members, etc.

Like the messages of most marketing vehicles, AIDA applies to e-mail. Grabbing the reader's attention, as always, is key. First, your e-mail subject line should be unique or compelling; your goal is to entice the receiver to open it. Special offers or exciting news can be good subject line topics. Try to create a sense of urgency. If appropriate, use a limited time sales promotion or special information giveaway, such as a white paper on a related subject. Use your brand name in the "From" line so you'll be recognized or remembered quickly. Certainly try to pique the reader's interest and create desire. Telling the readers what they'll miss if they don't respond is always a good way to do that.

Of course, you must ask for action. You can ask the recipient to respond to order a product, visit a website, provide comments or ask for more information. If you get a comment or question, be sure to reply quickly.

All of this must be done in short order. Keep your e-mail short, both in length and message. If the content goes beyond one screen, you may lose your reader's interest. Here's an example of a single screen, e-mail newsletter that my agency produces monthly to promote Crosby Marketing, our clients, and their causes. This issue of the newsletter features a campaign for the U.S. Department of Agriculture.

CROSBYCONNECTS

ISSUE 11, VOL 1

Engaging millions to promise to protect America's forests.

The USDA came to Crosby with a killer problem. The Emerald Ash Borer beetle had invaded our forests, causing devastation and destroying millions of trees. Our task was to motivate immediate action to help stop the bug from spreading.

With the emotional appeal of the "Promise" campaign, viewers are powerfully compelled to make a promise not to move firewood, which spreads the beetle. The campaign creative was tested prior to release, and we heard firsthand from consumers that they appreciated and connected with the positive appeal from the USDA.

The fully integrated campaign kicked off mid-May in 13 states with TV, radio and print PSAs, paid outdoor on key travel routes and web banners on sites such as Weather.com and MapQuest, along with a campaign microsite and extensive media relations.

The USDA wanted powerful exposure to help support each state's grassroots efforts. So far, the campaign has earned equivalent media value in excess of $4 million with over 550 million impressions and 50,000 web visits to the microsite, exceeding all expectations.

SEE THE COMPLETE USDA CAMPAIGN

"The results have been outstanding because of the consistent, integrated nature of the campaign. Every element was well executed and powerfully delivered through a media mix that really works."
Sharon Lucik,
Public Affairs Specialist
United States Department of Agriculture Animal & Plant Health Inspection Service

Miss Our Last Edition?
Read It Here »

Follow Crosby On:

Visit Crosby website   Contact us   Other News

E-mail remains one of the most important marketing applications of the Internet, though it would have to share that crown with the website—the other star of Web 1.0.

Web 1.0 to Web 2.0

The label "Web 1.0" is called a "retronym," a word coined in the
1980s to describe something that differentiates the original version of it
from a more recent version, in this case "Web 2.0." For example, if
George W. Bush hadn't been elected President, there would have been
no need for calling his father, George H.W. Bush, "Bush One." If we
hadn't had World War II, we wouldn't have reclassified "the great war"
of 1914-18 as "WWI."

In effect, Web 1.0 was the progenitor or sire of Web 2.0. Web 1.0
has no hard and fast parameters, but it is defined mostly by the website.
Web 1.0 featured the read-only, static website that allowed you to find
information online about a person or organization but offered minimal
interaction with the site.

Even a static website is better than none at all. Having a website is
like having your office or store open 24 hours a day, seven days a week.
You can be seen at any time and, therefore, you're marketing every
minute of every day. For example, I don't recall a recent new business
discussion with a prospect or a conversation with a prospective hire
where the person didn't indicate he or she checked out our website in
advance. Also, there's hardly an ad, newsletter, or news release we create for clients that doesn't have a website address as a call to action.

Technological refinements that produced new Internet-based software applications brought about Web 2.0. These applications allowed
organizations not only to communicate with their customers but to get
feedback as well.

Web 2.0 is best described as the "participatory web." Anyone can
participate online and influence the conversation. Thus, Web 2.0 allows
groups of people to exchange information and ideas, transforming the
Internet from a static information source to a dynamic knowledge-shar-
ing tool.

While there is no single event heralding the change from Web 1.0 to
Web 2.0, the blog (short for "weblog") is a symbolic, transitional website that allows for interactivity. While there were earlier bulletin-board-
like Internet sites, the modern blog began to proliferate in the early
2000s. Today, there are more than one-hundred million blogs around the
world.

Blogging can benefit your business in several ways. Blogs can be used to market your products or services, build your brand both internally and externally, or send important information to various audiences. You can even place ads for your offerings on your own blogs. As for outside media, other people's blogs that reach your target audience can spread your word through PR messages you supply or ads you buy on these blogs. Even mainstream journalists' blogs may be receptive to your news.

In a *New York Times* article back in December, 2007, I found a great example of a small business that successfully used a variety of blogging techniques. The business was Denali Flavors, an ice cream manufacturing company in Michigan that licenses its flavors to other stores. A small company with a limited ad budget, Denali Flavors used a series of blogs to build brand awareness for Moose Tracks, its most popular ice cream flavor. As Marci Alboher, author of the article, reported:

> *"John Nardini, who runs marketing for Denali and is responsible for the company's blogs, said he has experimented over the last few years with different types of blogs to see which would generate the most traffic. One blog followed a Denali-sponsored bicycle team that was raising money for an orphanage in Latvia. Another tracked the whereabouts of a moose character that would show up at famous landmarks around the country.*

> *"But by far the most successful blog, in terms of traffic, turned out to be Free Money Finance, a blog that has nothing to do with Denali's business. Mr. Nardini's plan was to create a blog with so much traffic that it could serve as an independent media outlet owned by Denali Flavors, where the company could be the sole sponsor and advertiser. He chose personal finance because it is a popular search category on the web and because he knew he would not tire of posting about it. And post he does, about five times each weekday.*

> *"He uses free tools like Google Analytics and Site Meter to understand how people are finding the site and which key words are working. Free Money Finance receives about 4,500 visits a day and each visitor views about two pages, which means they see two ads for Moose Tracks ice cream. The effort costs about $400 a year, excluding Mr. Nardini's salary.*

> *"This site also accepts advertising, which earns the company about $30,000 to $40,000 a year, all of which Denali donates to charity."*

Online, Especially, It's The Customer, Stupid!

Between e-mail, websites, and blogging, marketers have powerful online marketing tools literally at their fingertips, and we haven't yet scratched the surface of Web 2.0. The opportunities in online marketing are so vast and so dynamic that, as I approached writing this chapter, I wondered how to get it all in. Then it hit me. It's The Customer, Stupid! For the marketer, it's not about the ever-expanding technology with its myriad appliances and applications. It's all about marketing, and marketing is all about the customer. Despite the newness of the Internet, those words written by Peter Drucker more than half a century ago are as true as ever: Marketing is "the whole business seen from the point of view of its final result; that is from the customer's point of view."

This truism was confirmed by one of today's technology gurus, Jeff Bezos, founder of Amazon, which has revolutionized retailing and reading. He credits Amazon's success to starting from the customer's point of view, not with the service or product. In a January, 2010, *Newsweek* interview, Daniel Lyons asked Bezos, "How do you define what Amazon is today?" "We start with the customer and we work backward," Bezos replied. "We learn whatever skills we need to service the customer. We build whatever technology we need to service the customer."

Bezos calls the very successful Kindle ebook reading device an example of working backward from the customer. He doesn't disparage a business' approach to taking a set of skills and determining what else you can do with them. On the contrary, he says that's one useful way to extend what you're doing. But he prefers the customer first method. In the *Newsweek* interview, he explained: "Rather than ask what are we good at and what else can we do with that skill, you ask, who are our customers? What do they need? And then you say we're going to give that to them regardless of whether we currently have the skills to do so, and we will learn those skills no matter how long it takes. Kindle is a great example of that."

That method certainly worked for Bezos. The Kindle has become Amazon's number one best selling product.

No matter what technique you use, marketing seeks a result from a customer. In the Internet age that may be more important than ever because now the roles of marketer and customer are often reversed, with the customer initiating the buying process.

My friend and mentor Tony Mikes, founder of the global, independent 1,000 member advertising agency network called Second Wind, explains it this way:

> *"Not so long ago, marketers talked about being 'consumer-centric.' But marketers remained in charge of what was 'central.' The consumer makes that choice today. Businesses and marketing firms that fail to adapt to this flipped relationship will go the way of the dinosaurs."*

Tony, a former ad agency owner, has been following the Internet impact for the last 15 years. As one of his early members, we at Crosby Marketing have been following it with him. In his *Second Wind Newsletter*, Tony wrote a piece that sums up the move from Web 1.0 to Web 2.0. Under the heading "What Do We Mean by 'New Media,'" he wrote:

> *"Not so very long ago, 'new media' meant the Internet. Then it grew to include e-commerce, online advertising, and e-marketing. But that was Web 1.0. When we say 'new media' today, it is Web 2.0 we speak of. This generation of media options includes a host of CGM-driven elements: (CGM = Customer-Generated Marketing)*
>
> *• Blogs*
> *• Video*
> *• Mobile*
> *• Podcasting*
> *• Webcasting*
> *• Wiki*
> *• Social networking*
> *• Viral e-mail*
> *• Text messaging*
>
> *"The common element in all of these channels is the consumer. The end user has moved front and center, and now claims the attention of marketers worldwide. New media participants are not only changing marketing (and the larger Internet) as we know it, they are hugely influential, at the forefront of changing trends, and terrifyingly collaborative. The Internet and related networking capabilities allows them to organize within hours to 'flame' a company's e-mail server, spread news (true or false) across blogs worldwide, and text-message to a huge circle of 'friends' through Smartphones and mobile technology . . . who then text all of their friends, who text their friends . . . .*

"How do you protect your brands and deliver ad messages in a digital environment that doubles as a 'wide open town'? The new media rules are, there are no rules. Yet consumers continue to move away from traditional media. Mass marketing no longer reaches the majority of the masses. Marketers want, and need, to reach out to the new media users to balance these mass-marketing losses."

We can see the shift of marketing to new media in our business. Every client and prospect conversation now has an online marketing component. Therefore, Crosby Marketing, like other marketing companies, from tiny shops to huge ad agency conglomerates, have established online or interactive departments or subsidiaries. Spending on websites, web ads, search engine optimization, etc. has taken a huge chunk out of traditional mass media ad spending.

Reaching out to new media users has also caused a shift from the impersonal mass media approach to almost an old-fashioned, corner grocer kind of person-to-person marketing—only with the rapid speed and fantastic reach of the Internet.

Tony Mikes is among the many marketing pros who recognized that the end user once more has moved front and center of marketing. For example, Sergio Zyman and Scott Miller in their book, *Building Brandwidth*, discussed it at length, concluding, "On the Net, customization rules. Internet companies accept a key principle ignored by many other marketers: Fixate on the customer, not on the product or the competition." Likewise, David Corkindale, writing in the *New York Times* in 2008, noted the shift in conventional marketing wisdom from the customer as the hunted to becoming the hunter.

He labeled as a fallacy the old idea that "Marketing is all about hunting and capturing clients." "No, not anymore," he wrote. "These days, in the Internet Age, marketing is sometimes about the company being the prey.

"The role of marketers has long been to hunt out clients and, with the aid of salespeople, capture this prey. However, particularly with the maturation of the Internet, the tide is turning.

"For instance, in the vacation market now, many people hunt out the holiday they want themselves. They use the Internet to find and then make choices, sometimes interrogating potential sellers online. In industries like this, the role of marketing is to make sure that a company's products or services are easily found online, and that the company responds effectively to potential customers."

The point is that today's online customers are not passive receivers of your marketing actions and messages. They are active participants. Therefore, you must be ready for them before they reach you. Remember, the customer is only a mouse click away from your (or your competitor's) product, service, or message. Often it is the customer who seeks out your site, reads your e-mail, or follows your blog. That online customer could be searching for you online at the specific time he or she wants what you have to offer. That's an opportunity not to be missed.

Optimizing for Search Engines

"I'll Google it" has become almost a universal term for searching for information online. In fact, search engines such as Google, YouTube, and Yahoo are the pathfinders in the Internet's tangled forest. Customers finding websites online has become known as "inbound" marketing. Customers may need help finding you online, so optimizing your position on search engines becomes a critical marketing tool. It's so important for our clients, for example, my agency has a full team dedicated to search engine marketing (SEM) and search engine optimization (SEO).

Like many of the new online/Internet/interactive techniques, search has a schizophrenic identity. "Search engine marketing" is used by some as a generic term for all marketing activities connected to search, and they use "search engine optimization" as just one of those activities. However, most online specialists differentiate the two monetarily, with SEM being paid search marketing and SEO being free or "natural." In that vein, definitions used by the AAAAs is pertinent:

"Search Engine Marketing: A form of Internet Marketing that seeks to promote websites by increasing their visibility in the Search Engine result pages.

"Search Engine Optimization: The process of improving the volume and quality of traffic to a website from search engines via 'natural' ('organic' or 'algorithmic') search results."

Paid SEM gives you the opportunity to "pay-per-click," paying the search engine company a certain amount of money for each person who visits your site from its engine. These "sponsored links" can put you in the top few online listings in your category. The positives about paid listings are that you only pay for performance, you can get immediate results, and, because search engines track the clicks, your marketing is much more quantifiable.

Generally speaking, search engines rank websites based on a mathematical formula, an algorithm that measures the use of key words in the text, meta-tags, and backlinks. If you leave your positioning to the search engine, there's no telling how far down you'll be in the list of your category. Therefore, optimizing your website for search engines can make you more prominent, increasing your chance to be selected by the searcher.

SEO leads are considered very high quality for several reasons. SEO helps position your website for the customer who is looking for what you have to offer. Thus it prequalifies the searching prospect. In addition, many searchers realize that the top, segmented listings are probably paid for and may view them more like advertising than as an information source.

When you can't or don't want to pay for sponsoring links, you need to optimize your position naturally, although there's nothing natural about it. It's almost a scientific exercise.

To explain a complex subject in simple terms, the mathematical formula used by search engines deals with text only and the keywords and meta-tags it contains. The keywords are those words and phrases the searcher will use to find you. This requires some research since what the organization says about itself may not be words the searcher looks for.

For example, a client of ours defined its top keywords as "International Travel Insurance." It made sense to the company because that's how its competitors defined themselves. However, our research, using a program that allows you to learn what people are searching for, found that the top searcher-defined keywords in the category were:

• Medical Travel Insurance
• Travel Health Insurance
• Travel Abroad Insurance
• Worldwide Travel Insurance

The more relevant the content keywords are on your website, the more search engines will consider it a resource in your category. Links to your site (backlinks) from other "trusted" websites also raise your popularity among search engines.

Another important factor in search engine rankings are the meta-tags. Meta-tags are parts of the HTML code used to build websites, and they tell search engines what the web page is about.

Herein lies the conundrum of SEO. While SEO leads to free, higher positioning on search engines, it takes a knowledgeable professional to do it right—to ensure the appearance and position of proper keywords and meta-tags. Suddenly a "free" listing costs you the salary or fees of a professional. It certainly will be worth it if it puts you on the first page of the search engine results.

The other negatives of SEO, as compared to SEM: Tracking statistics are minimal, and there can be a six-to-twelve-month lag time before the search engines pick up your keywords.

Despite the costs and other barriers, optimizing your website position—by SEM or SEO—will drive highly qualified people to your website, and there aren't many things more important in marketing than a captured customer.

Content Is King

Once the customer learns where your site is on the Internet, you want him or her to return often so you can continue to build your relationship, i.e., brand loyalty. Therefore, your website content is critical. If it stays the same, customer visit after customer visit, the customer will get bored and stop visiting. Give the customers something fresh to see when they return and flag it on your homepage.

Changing content will stimulate interest, as scientists have discovered. As an example, they cite the placement of mobiles over babies' cribs. Few parents read the instructions for installing a mobile for their infant. But, if they did, they would note the direction to change the mobile's position around the crib every few days. This difference in positioning will stimulate the baby's brain to process the change and consider it in a new way. In the same manner, organizations have to keep their websites dynamic and current so that visitors don't become conditioned to them and ignore the messaging.

Once customers are at your site, it's content that will keep them there. New and interesting content will help customers stick around. That's what online marketers call the site's "stickiness,"—an actual measure of the duration of the visitor's visit and, therefore, a way to judge the site's effectiveness. The longer visitors stay on your site, the more chance you have to earn their trust, build loyalty, or make a "sale."

As Second Wind's Tony Mikes told me: "Companies must strive to be perceived as part of the consumer's community of reliable resources —to become trusted insiders, not just somebody selling something. This is why content is now king. Quality content is a company's entree into the consumer's world. This content driven relationship is needed because most consumers today trust their friends more than they trust companies or marketers. Trusted content enables the company to reestablish credibility and build stronger, longer-lasting relationships. Of course, it goes without saying that the content must be truthful. Today's customer is very smart. Any attempt to mislead or obfuscate by the company will lead to mistrust or worse—disqualification."

That doesn't mean you don't target your information at the customers' wants or needs—and ensure it promotes your offering—but customers are looking for advice to help them make informed decisions, not hard-selling advertising or PR fluff. Quality online content builds brand loyalty, moves customers to action, and brings them back for more. Your content must be easy to understand and easy to access. In a sense, online you must act more like a journalist than a marketer. Also, quality content can differentiate you from competitors who may be on the customer's search list as well.

Some marketers call this informational approach a "pull" concept, whereby you draw in your customers rather than "pushing" your product or service at them through promotion. However, you can't rely solely on a "pull" concept in marketing. Often, in order to pull you have to push. You must make customers aware of your product, service, or organization. While the mass media form of push may be inefficient, perhaps even obsolete, if used only by itself, the offline ad, news release, newsletter, etc., remain important parts of moving customers to action, especially if you want them to find you online. (See Chapter XI) E-mail, blogs, and other online methods still "push" messages into the marketplace. In addition, many organizations even use push marketing on social media, such as Facebook, Twitter, MySpace, and others, to offer information and instruction.

Social Networking

The growth of social media has added a whole new dimension to online marketing. It has intensified online participation of the customer in an organization's communications and public relations. The number of worldwide Internet users visiting social networks exceeds 500 million. As social network activity expands, so will social network marketing. For marketers, social networking allows them to join customers' conversations in a space the customer already occupies. You can talk to customers, listen to them, teach them, learn from them. You can even have them selling for you.

Social networks harken back to the most basic—and probably the most effective form of marketing, word-of-mouth. You can share content with your online friends, and they can share that content with their "friends," thereby becoming salespersons for you. It's viral marketing at its best, where your story gets passed on from person to person. An example of this was the DuPont Company's use of its dramatic product test and demonstration film footage, showing race-car crashes, policemen's vests stopping bullets and exploding oil refineries, in a social media strategy to reach young professionals via viral video. The footage was turned into a series of three-minute programs and successfully distributed widely across online video sites because of its uniqueness.

For organizations, the added value of participating in social networking is what they can learn by listening. Customers' thoughts and ideas about products, services, or activities can help organizations modify their marketing strategies or tactics—even their product design. Dell, the computer company, when following customers' Twitter feeds, noticed complaints about certain of its laptop computer keys being too close together. Dell fixed the problem on its next generation laptop.

Thus, social media has become what one writer called a "giant focus group." Like Dell, you must be monitoring social media conversations to feel the pulse of customers. Monitoring these conversations provides an early warning system. You can react quickly to rebut erroneous information or fix a problem before it becomes a crisis. For example, at Southwest Airlines, there's a social media team that tracks Twitter comments, monitors a Facebook group, interacts with bloggers, and oversees the airline's presence on YouTube, Flickr, and LinkedIn.

Therein lies a problem created by social networking. The Internet has become a huge complaint box. As many a company has learned, agitated customers can turn mistakes and misunderstandings, real and imagined, into viral criticism. In recent times, for example, banks have been excoriated online for increases in credit card fees and service charges. Having a social media monitoring program is a must for most organizations.

The healthcare giant Johnson & Johnson learned its monitoring lesson when it launched a new online ad for its over-the-counter pain reliever Motrin. The commercial targeted moms who got back pain from carrying their babies in a sling. The ad created a storm of protests from Johnson & Johnson's top customers—moms—who thought the message trivialized women's pain and baby-carrying practices. Their complaints flooded blogs, YouTube, and Twitter. Johnson & Johnson yanked the ad and offered its apologies on the Motrin website and its online consumer blog. A Motrin spokesperson looked on the positive side of the flap, commenting, "One bright spot is that we learned through this process, in particular, the importance of paying close attention to the conversations that are taking place online."

The power of the consumer—moms in this case—was discussed on the Today show soon thereafter. Citing the Motrin ad example, Today show host Ann Curry asked Terri Walter, from the marketing company Razorfish, why advertisers want consumer feedback. Walter's response related the feedback to the "world of public relations." "Typically," she said, "brands would talk to journalists and would present them with their products and ask them to write about it. And they would have to . . . let them write either the good or the bad. Now, in the world of social media, moms and consumers are also having a voice. And so, it's very important for brands to understand who their influencers are and to figure out how to leverage that."

Of course, you can't leverage or monitor social media if you don't join it. At a minimum you should have a Facebook page, a Twitter account, a blog and be LinkedIn. If you want to see how we practice what I preach, look at the Crosby Connects e-mail newsletter earlier in this section. You'll see that it says you can "Follow Crosby" on *Facebook, Delicious, Twitter* and *LinkedIn* and gives you the symbols to link to them.

Having a Facebook page encourages customers to become fans and supports conversations over time. Twitter, on the other hand, because of its 140 character limit, is more of a real time tool. Twitter is good for grabbing a customer's attention and leading him or her to a more robust site, such as a newsletter or a blog. Twitter has become a useful customer service connection. I became acutely aware of the customer empowerment of social media when a Crosby colleague told me that's how he solved a problem with his Comcast Cable television reception. Instead of the usual phone call to a supplier with its interminable wait and potential passalong from one service rep to another, he simply tweeted Comcast (@comcastcares) and got immediate response and instruction.

The value of social media such as Twitter and Facebook is well documented for small business as well as large, as evidenced by this example from a 2009 *BusinessWeek* article:

> *"The connections you make in social networks are the primary value of spending time in social media. It's not the marketing or advertising that makes you money, it's the people you meet who refer you business, solve a problem for free (or for a fee), and drive attention and traffic your way. Until of course, enterprising business owners realize that being connected to a community can yield profit.*
>
> *"Enter Twitter as the ultimate traffic driver for retailers. Leave it to a small business owner to do this, but when a coffee shop/lounge owner in Houston decided to join Twitter, he didn't realize it would double his traffic. His store traffic, that is. For real.*
>
> *"When J.R. Cohen, Operations Manager for CoffeeGroundz (@coffeegroundz) Café in Houston, Texas first heard about Twitter from one of his customers, he was puzzled but intrigued. Today, he credits Twitter with almost doubling his clientele and with opening his eyes to a whole new way to build community.*
>
> *"What's interesting about this is the owner just joined to make friends, and the business aspect happened as a natural outgrowth of his success in becoming a personality online. Once a customer was comfortable that he would be reached, the customer asked a question about business, and the result was a 'slap yourself in the head and say why didn't I think of it' moment."*

At Crosby Marketing, we're also making professional friends through the business-oriented social networking site *LinkedIn*. In 2010, *LinkedIn* had more than 50 million registered users maintaining contacts with people—called connections—they know and trust in business.

These connections exchange information, ideas, and opportunities for new business. In that way, *connections* are customers, too.

The secret to marketing success on social media is participation. Engagement with your "friends" and regular activity is essential. No one on Facebook, Twitter, LinkedIn, etc., enjoys having a one-way conversation, receiving unsolicited marketing information, viewing an inactive site that remains unchanged, or receiving no response to inquiries. Such a site is a bit like the rotten fish example from an earlier chapter. Selling conversation and delivering silence will harm your marketing efforts, not help them. That's a reminder of an earlier lesson we learned, that marketing requires consistent, meaningful communications. Remember, too, that in social media, content is king. Consistent, quality content will ensure engagement with your customers.

If you are engaged with your social media followers, it's easier to share information about your product, service, or cause. That makes it more probable that your web "friends" will share your message virally, especially if the content is new, interesting, unique, or motivational. Social media also allows you to link your "friends" to your website to find more information or link them to other sites that support your offering.

The corollary to sharing your message on social media is listening carefully to the conversation, not just conversations with you but those of your followers and their "friends." How they talk to each other about you and your offering can be extremely revealing. Their conversation will let you know what matters to them. As noted earlier, in the case of Dell's too close computer keys, even negative feedback can be constructive, if you have an open mind as well as open ears.

The next lesson on social media is—you must keep up. The fast-moving world of the web has become hand-held and mobile, and your marketing must move forward. As I tell my staff, in the marketing world, we're like the French Foreign Legion. Their mantra was "March or Die." Ours is "Grow or Die."

Mobile Marketing
The cell phone, morphing increasingly into smartphone form, has entered the already rousing social media field. With more cell phones in use than landline phones, mobile devices present a great marketing opportunity and the ultimate in person-to-person communication. Mobile phones and pads, with their growing number of applications,

appear to be the marketing communications vehicle of the future. I say "appear to be" on purpose.

There are many barriers to overcome to make these phones a marketing Mecca. Marketers are still sorting out how organizations can reach specific target audiences through mobile. How do you tailor messages for the mobile audience and deliver it on a small screen? How does the receiver differentiate your marketing messages from spam? How many potential customers will use mobile for commerce?

Despite such issues, mobile and its growing number of applications can't be avoided, not when you'll find the tool in so many pockets or purses. As suggested by Cristy Burgan, Vice President for Marketing Solutions at Acision, a mobile specialist company, in an article for the Mobile Marketing Association:

> *"This new channel reaches out to the end user's most personal of devices, the one they consider a necessity. As such, advertisements delivered to the mobile device must have purpose and reason without being intrusive. It is only when delivered appropriately that the medium will reach its full potential.*

> *"Messaging is the most widely used and understood data channel. Gaining a customer's permission to send messaging-based ads/promotions from brands, products, and services of their choice unlocks the largest, most interactive marketing advertising channel. Delivering ads based on a customer's preference creates relevance which in turn will drive increased response rates and customer satisfaction.*

> *"Marketers and operators have a responsibility to ensure that mobile advertising does not morph into another spam machine much in the same way that e-mail advertising has evolved. The mobile phone offers an unmatched channel for delivering content-rich, interactive and targeted promotions/services; it is a marketer's dream, but it must be handled responsibly or risks alienating consumers."*

While many mobile users wouldn't want to receive unsolicited advertising on their phones, some have already signed up to view ads in exchange for free cell minutes or free video content. Free offers are one of many of ways to get customers' agreement to accept mobile marketing messages. As Cristy Burgan suggests:

"There is a need to overcome the potential barriers regarding customer acceptance. This can be achieved by ensuring the user feels in control of his/her advertising experience by easily being able to opt-in and opt-out of any campaign, determining the number of advertisements they will receive and benefiting from an incentive or reward for participating. In addition to this, users must receive relevant ads that deliver value to them in their everyday lives. If this is done well, everyone benefits."

Mobile marketing, as with other social networking, offers more than advertising opportunities. It's a great way to create word-of-mouth (or word-by-phone) through text messaging or sharing applications by users. This is especially true among the largest cohorts of mobile users, teens and young adults, giving marketers great access to these demographic targets.

A good example of targeting and engaging such customers was a mobile marketing campaign my agency produced for a client, Kaiser Permanente. In a 2009 mobile campaign we called "Turn Your Cell Phone Into A Well Phone," Kaiser wanted to target federal employees in the Washington, D.C., area with special emphasis on young employees age 25-34.

To build a highly targeted database of these young "health-seeking" Federal employees for Kaiser, Crosby Marketing launched the "Mobile Wellness Coach." This opt-in program delivered daily health tips, recipes, and more directly to Federal employees' cell phones. To broaden the appeal of the initiative, each week carried a unique theme (exercise, lung health, chronic disease prevention, work/life balance, etc.). We utilized a format that included wellness tips, jokes, recipes, and inspirational quotes—all designed to reinforce the brand's "thrive" focus on a healthy body, mind, and spirit. In just three months, the campaign generated nearly 1,000 new Kaiser Permanente prospects. Just as important, a fully automated system allows Kaiser to communicate with these prospects via their cell phones for ongoing marketing and relationship building.

Marketing departments in large companies such as Visa and Starbucks use mobile marketing campaigns, but small businesses have gotten into the act, especially by building a database of customer cell phone numbers. The *Wall Street Journal*, for example, reported "smartphone applications have changed the way many small businesses operate. Now more firms are turning to these apps to enhance the way customers interact with their products and services—and even boost their bottom lines."

Being a placeholder in customers' smartphones means you go wherever the phone goes. There are many smartphone app developers and development kits available, which can build you an app for a few hundred or a few thousand dollars.

Mobile marketing and coming generation smartphones appear to be the next leap forward in online marketing, creating a pathway to Web 3.0.

What some are calling Web 3.0, the next level of person-to-person marketing, promises to offer online applications that enhance computer-to-computer interactivity, whether the vehicle is a personal computer, a mobile phone, or some newer whiz-bang, electronic apparatus or application.

Since Web 3.0 is a retronym of Web 2.0, and we're not there yet, the expectations for its makeup are varied. Certainly it will have enhanced interactivity and enhanced content to share. Some see it as the Internet handling tasks that now require human direction, such as finding, sharing, and combining information. Others see it in terms of an unbelievable data resource at your fingertips. For example, *BusinessWeek* magazine reports that some companies already are using a cutting edge technology that merges virtual reality with real-world images, called "augmented reality," in an effort to engage audiences more deeply in social media. The neatest definition I have seen of Web 3.0 is, "Even cooler than Web 2.0." Whatever it becomes will be a brave new world for marketers.

But the brave new world doesn't mean the old world is dead. There are warnings from marketing pros, and I count myself among them, that while social marketing is a must, don't jump on its bandwagon to the detriment of more basic online marketing. For example, e-mail marketing will remain a universal communications tool, and e-mail is still improving. At this writing, I have a technological genius friend diligently working on a way you'll be able to rid your e-mail of spam. Online advertising will continue to grow, and search programs will get better and faster. I have seen predictions that by 2015 banner advertising will be five times larger than social media and search marketing will be 10 times larger.

I can take the caveat to a brave new world one step further. Despite the growth of online marketing, it would be foolish to jump on its bandwagon to the exclusion of traditional marketing techniques, as the next chapter will prove.

Glossary of Social Media and Online Marketing Terms

Social media terms and techniques every organization manager and marketer should understand:

Social Network: An online destination, such as a blog, Facebook page, or Twitter account, that gives users a chance to connect with one or more groups of "friends," facilitating sharing of content, news, and information among them. Social network sites and communities have user-centric content and interactive features.

Social Marketing: The marketing tactic that taps into the growth of social networks, encouraging users to pass along information or content created by an organization or to add its brand to the users' social circle of friends or contacts.

Social Networking: In the online world, social networking describes the way users build online networks of contacts and interact with these personal or business friends in a secure environment. These types of sites, such as MySpace, allow you to link to others to share information, insights, and experiences.

Search Engines: A web search engine is a tool that allows you to search for information on the web using keywords. Results of the search containing these keywords are usually presented in a list. The information may consist of web pages, images, and other types of files. Some popular search engines have been Google, Yahoo, and Bing.

Search Engine Optimization (SEO): The process of improving the volume or quality of traffic to a website by making its content highly relevant to search engines and searchers via "natural" (organic or algorithmic) search results. Tactics for placing a company or individual website high on results lists are important for organizations to consider as they develop and maintain their websites and related links.

Search Engine Marketing (SEM): Most online specialists use "search engine marketing" to denote paid search as opposed to SEO's "natural" results. These "sponsored links" or "pay per click" guarantee your listing is high on the search list.

RSS Feed: Also known as and *XML feed, syndicated content,* or *web feed,* an RSS feed is frequently updated content published by a website. It is usually used for news and blog sites, but can also be used for distributing other types of digital content, including pictures, audio, or video.

Text Messaging: The process of sending brief written messages (texts) between mobile phones, over cellular networks.

Viral E-mail: A type of e-mail that rapidly propagates from person to person, generally in a word of mouth manner. The process usually involves an individual receiving an e-mail that he or she forwards to friends/contacts. They in turn, forward the e-mail to a group of friends, thus spreading the content rapidly, potentially in large-scale proportions.

Blogs: Blog is the short term for Web Log. A blog is essentially a publicly accessible online journal that is frequently updated by a particular individual or organization regarding a specific topic. The action of updating a blog is called blogging. Blog postings can be formal or informal, depending on who's generating the content. Blogs are the foundation for any social media marketing campaign and crucial for search engine optimization. Creating new content and posting it on blogs on a regular basis will help organizations remain prominent in the search engine rankings. If you have a static website and no other content online, yours may not be found easily.

Podcast: A method of publishing audio or video broadcasts via the Internet. Allows users to subscribe to a feed of new files (usually MP3s). Podcasts became popular due largely to automatic downloading of audio content onto portable media players (like the iPod) or personal computers.

Wiki: A wiki is a page or collection of Web pages designed to enable anyone who accesses it to contribute or modify content. Wikis are often used to create a collaborative website and to power community websites. The collaborative encyclopedia Wikipedia is one of the best-known Wikis. Wikis can be used to allow people to write a document together or to share reference materials that let colleagues or even members of the public contribute content.

Facebook: Facebook is a free-access social networking website that is operated and privately owned by Facebook, Inc. Users can join networks organized by interest, workplace, school, or region to connect and interact with other people. Company Facebook pages offer a unique company presence where users can become more deeply connected with a business or brand. In addition to creating their own Facebook page(s), businesses can advertise on Facebook to a very targeted audience.

Twitter: Twitter is a "micro blogging" site. It is basically an online community where people share short, text-based (140 characters or less) messages/posts, primarily for self-promotion. Twitter posts, or "tweets," are widespread among media and text users and have become useful to organizations for marketing and customer service.

MySpace: MySpace is the prototypical example of a social networking site. MySpace is promoted as an online community that lets you meet your friends' friends and create a private community where you can share photos, journals, and information with a growing network of friends.

LinkedIn: LinkedIn groups are the business networking site's equivalent of a Facebook page. More than 50 million professionals use LinkedIn, the business professionals' social network, to exchange information, ideas, and opportunities. It allows the user to find communities of professionals who share a common experience, interest, affiliation, or goal.

YouTube: YouTube is a video sharing website on which users can upload and share videos. There is a wide variety of user-generated video content, including movie clips, TV clips, and music videos, as well as amateur content such as video blogging and short original videos. While most of the content is uploaded by individuals, organizations offer some of their marketing material via the site.

Flickr: Flickr is an image and video hosting website, web services suite, and online community platform. In addition to being a popular website for users to share personal photographs, the service is widely used by bloggers as a photo repository. When you post pictures to Flickr, you can also link viewers to your website, which can be a good promotional tool.

Application Programming Interface (API): An interface that allows one software program to interact with others. The publishing of APIs has given web communities the ability to create an open architecture for sharing of content and data. For example, content created in one place can be dynamically posted and/or updated in multiple online locations—photos can be shared from sites like Flickr to social network sites such as Facebook and MySpace. Or, comments made on Twitter can be posted to a Facebook account because of APIs on those sites.

CHAPTER 11

A Marriage Made in Marketing Heaven

———⊰◇⊱———

New Media + Old Media = The Future of Marketing

In 2009, a dowdy, unassuming woman named Susan Boyle, from a tiny town in Scotland, appeared on the reality show "Britain's Got Talent" and shocked the judges and the audience with her gifted voice. Her performance went viral on the Internet, producing millions of hits and making Ms. Boyle a celebrity and commercial success. This event also showed the uncommon value of the marriage between offline and online media, as reported in the *Washington Post*:

> *"To media observers, the speed and scope of Boyle's online ubiquity is a testament that the marriage between old media (her performance first aired on British television) and new media (it then made its way to YouTube, Twitter, and Facebook) is broadening the reach of all media, from one channel to another, from person to person."*

Thanks to the *Post* for supplying the definition of where I believe marketing is heading: "The marriage between old media and new media is broadening the reach of all media, from one channel to another, from person to person."

The value of television in that equation also calls into question the prediction that old media is dying. While traditional media has faced some advertising and online competitive woes, like Mark Twain said of his premature obituary, reports of its death are greatly exaggerated.

At this writing, certainly major daily newspaper reading and revenues have diminished, but niche magazines such as *Vanity Fair* are as thick with ads as ever. While it has lost ad revenue, television is watched by more Americans than ever before, and cable TV is among the leaders in media revenue growth. Outdoor advertising, mainly billboards, is a much-used media. Radio advertising is down, but as long as automobiles exist, there will be marketers who will pay for programming. And, as useful a communications tool as it has become, e-mail marketing hasn't put much of a dent in direct mail, as your mail box will attest.

It is also significant to realize that among adult Internet users, traditional media formats, such as network and local TV news, get more of adults' time than Internet sites, blogs, or social networks.

In no way does that diminish the marketing value of new media. The truth is that by adding new media to old media, we now have a marketing universe overflowing with channels through which to engage our customers. We have new ways to market our products, services, and organizations, but the marketing purpose itself is not new—build the brand, sell the product, engage the customer. In few cases can an organization do this with new media alone, and with so many marketing options available, why should they?

True, my daughter-in-law does most of her furniture and fixture shopping online. Seldom does she need a store or salesman to make a large purchasing decision. All she needs is a computer. On the other hand, I recently left my new fitness center, which I learned about from a direct mail offer, and saw a poster for a new Japanese restaurant around the corner, which I dined at later in the week. I didn't need a computer or smartphone to help me make either of those buying decisions. So strictly online or offline marketing can work in different situations.

But the most successful marketing now uses multiple channels of media to create a variety of touch points with the customer. More and more, a variety of channels work together to drive the customer to action. To get the best returns from marketing campaigns, the touch points will be from a mix of both traditional media and new media.

It's All Media

To quote Tim Williams, president of Ignition Consulting Group, who we have used to guide my firm on a brand positioning program, "It's all media." Tim explains that there are "bought media," such as mass media advertising or online advertising; even the display of products in stores can be bought media. There are "earned media," such as the article about you in a newspaper or on a blog, or your viral video on YouTube. Finally, there are "owned media," such as your brand's website and other online properties, your employees, especially salespeople, and your product itself. These are all customer touch points you have at your disposal.

Therefore, when you put together a marketing campaign, you must coordinate "all media," paid, earned, and owned. You can see how that's done in this case history for one of my firm's client campaigns.

Case History

"ForYourMarriage.org"—Crosby Marketing's Multimedia Catholic Communications Campaign

Recent trends led our client, the United States Conference of Catholic Bishops (USCCB), to one conclusion: it's time to communicate to the general public, and especially married couples and those considering marriage, the benefits of a healthy marriage.

In planning the campaign, we initially conducted one-on-one interviews with ten national experts on marriage to gather input for the development of a public service campaign. Then, we conducted focus groups among the general public to assess attitudes towards marriage and test potential campaign themes and messages.

In the focus groups, the simple question "What have you done for your marriage today?" got everyone to open up. Then, people-on-the-street interviews served as the basis for the multimedia public service campaign that highlights the importance that everyday actions hold for a healthy marriage and invited viewers and listeners to seek out information to strengthen their marriages at ForYourMarriage.org. The website address, which serves as the call to action of the campaign, is populated with articles, advice columns, and daily tips for educating and inspiring the public to put effort into their marriages every day.

The multimedia approach used a traditional PSA campaign to drive response. We used television and radio spots as "discussion starters" on the subject. They aired about 150,000 times nationally, earning the equivalent media value of more than $12 million in a single year. The spots were based on the people-on-the-street interviews. With cameras rolling, we asked people across America, "What have you done for your marriage today?" The answers are insightful, truthful, funny, profound, inspiring, and above all—real. The closing message invites the viewer to visit ForYourMarriage.org for helpful tips about strengthening marriage.

The online sources for more information and help were very robust, including the following tactics:

- The website, www.ForYourMarriage.org, provided resources for those looking for help strengthening their marriages, highlighted the public service campaign, and offered daily inspiration.

- An interactive locator tool on the website allowed people to locate marriage help in their area.

- A blog about a young woman preparing for marriage was provided by various news feeds to interested viewers.

- A For Your Marriage fan page was produced on Facebook where the television spots and daily marriage tips were posted.

- An e-mail newsletter was developed that provided interested website viewers with updates about new materials that were available online.

In its original stage, ForYourMarriage.org received more than 500,000 visitors and 2 million page views, and the e-mail newsletter is received by thousands of subscribers each month. Website visits have been bolstered by press coverage in secular and religious publications. It's worth noting that one of the most popular search terms bringing visitors to the site is "What have you done for your marriage today?" further demonstrating the emotional power of that simple question.

Many of our client campaigns now use the "all media" approach. Another example is the Social Security Administration's "Retire Online" campaign. To educate target audiences about this program, we developed an outreach effort featuring a campaign spokesperson, actress Patty Duke, of *Miracle Worker* fame, who is of appropriate age to speak to those planning to retire or who are accessing social security benefits for the first time. The campaign featured Patty Duke in TV and radio PSAs, a satellite TV and radio media tour, and print and online advertising.

Print ads appeared in such magazines as *Reader's Digest, Newsweek, Time,* and *Kiplinger's Personal Finance,* my old employer. A paid search marketing campaign was launched on Google, Yahoo!, and MSN with strategic keyword selection. We leveraged Patty Duke TV spots via display advertising on financial content websites, such as CNNMoney.com, Yahoo! Finance, and AARP.org. It all added up to a very successful campaign generating awareness, educating target audiences, and driving traffic to SocialSecurity.gov to apply for retirement benefits.

The "Stop the Beetle" campaign, mentioned in Chapter 10, to get people to "promise" not to move firewood, thus halting the spread of the Emerald Ash Borer beetle, used a mixture of media also. Radio spots and a mobile billboard campaign encouraged people to make their own promise at a special micro site, www.stopthebeetle.info.

The fact is, in today's technology-based communications world, spending marketing dollars on new media without old media, and vice versa, is a potential waste of money. Take the famous and expensive Super Bowl ads, for example. The mass media approach of the past that got so much chatter would be worthless today without the new media connection. Super Bowl advertisers have started adding digital extensions to their TV ads. In 2009, for example, advertisers used the TV ads to cause a digital ripple effect. Budweiser's Canadian unit, Labatt Breweries, gave Quebec viewers watching the Super Bowl a chance to use their remotes to click on links embedded in Budweiser ads that would take them to a channel where they could watch longer versions of the ads. Such interactive technologies will take integrated marketing communications to a whole new level.

Integrated Marketing Communications

As Shakespeare wrote, "The past is prologue." In chapter six we discussed how we discovered the power of blending different techniques—Integrated Marketing Communications—could have more impact on the customer. We cited a definition of Integrated Marketing Communications (IMC) as, "The process of managing all sources of information about a product/service to which a customer or prospect is exposed that behaviorally moves the customer toward a sale and maintains customer loyalty." The marriage of new media and old media has created "IMC squared."

In conversations with clients, we often explain the new level of IMC with a chart similar to the one that follows:

Integrated Marketing Focuses on the Customer

For example, just building a website, which many organizations view as joining the online marketing world, is like putting a band-aid on a cut that needs stitches. It will help, but it won't do the total job needed.

A limited online approach won't start new and meaningful conversations with customers according to Martha Lindsay, CEO of Lindsay, Stone & Briggs, an ad agency specializing in jump-starting brands using brand-based consumer insights. Writing in *AdAge*, Ms. Lindsay made a convincing argument for an integrated media mix:

> *"Even if people know there's an opportunity to have a conversation with you—on Twitter or your blog, for instance—you can't expect them to engage given all the other demands on their time. You'll need a strategy that both gets them to know you exist and care so much that you exist, they'll become intrigued about conversing with you. This requires a strategy that integrates search optimization, media, message and contributions of content from consumers.*

"The right strategy begins with the end in mind: What message can work across multiple platforms and be scaled so quickly and broadly it can drive sufficient revenues to support a business model?

"Very few companies have the luxury to let conversations build slowly over time. And no business can afford to risk a high-waste and low-impact effort. More often than not, high-impact campaigns with reasonable returns don't materialize solely from online ads and social media. Traditional media must be a major component of the mix."

As an example, Ms. Lindsay noted that despite Nike's overwhelming response to the launch of its online campaigns, Nike brand directors said that to optimize online dialog, they still must jump-start initiatives with traditional media. "That's because traditional media can do what social media cannot:" she concluded, "aggressively interject messages into people's lives in a socially acceptable way."

In fact, many customers resist social media or avoid it, for one reason or another, e.g., fear of change, electronic illiteracy, laziness. Depending on your customer demographics, there may be far fewer social media users than traditional media users. Also, not many customers today refer to a single media channel in making a purchase decision. There probably is no single media channel to reach all your customers.

So, you must develop a marketing strategy that includes a mix of media appropriate for your customers. That means you must unite all of your media resources, paid, earned, and owned; coordinate internal and external communications; make sure your public relations and advertising are in sync; be sure your customer relations efforts are ready to respond to inquiries, and, most of all, integrate your offline and online marketing.

CHAPTER 12

The Ultimate Lesson

———◇———

Experience IS the Best Teacher, if You Learn from Your Mistakes

> **"A wise man learns from experience; a wiser man learns from the experience of others."** — Ancient Chinese Proverb

Throughout this book, you have read about people who have impacted my marketing education along the way—people such as the father of modern management, Peter Drucker; the philosopher and author, Os Guinness; and agency network founder, Tony Mikes. And you have read about the books that have influenced me, from Philip Kotler's famous marketing texts to Tom Peter's searches for excellence to Sergio Zyman's discussions of building brands online.

As the Chinese proverb instructs, wiser people learn from the experience of others. Actually, others' marketing knowledge became my experience. That is the beauty of learning. We learn from others' experiences as well as our own, and their experiences come in a multitude of forms—their writings, their advice, their teachings, and their day-to-day encounters with life and work. Thus, we are learning from an unlimited universe of experiences, which far outdistance our own limited world. Many of those learning experiences can be found in the books in the reading list at the end of this chapter. The list is a bibliography of some of my sources for this book.

We learn from others' successes and their failures, just as we learn from our own ups and downs. It's easy to learn from success, but more difficult to treat failure as an opportunity to learn. But wise people do, to quote one of them who made many mistakes but triumphed in the end:

> **"All men make mistakes, but only wise men learn from their mistakes."**   **– Winston Churchill**

I certainly have made my share of mistakes in marketing and, undoubtedly, learned from them the hard way. Those marketing mistakes go from the extreme of causing business failures to simple proofreading errors, which are less drastic but still can be costly.

Proofreading: The Once and Future Lesson

One of my first journalistic learning experiences had to do with proofreading, which was a job I held one summer in my college years at the local paper, *The Annapolis Evening Capital*. I remember proofing a typeset galley with a story about a Mr. Aas. When the paper came out, we realized I had missed the typographer's error of replacing the second "a" in Mr. Aas' name with an "s." Needless to say, it made an ass out of me.

While I carried the fear of typos into the marketing business, we have had to reprint a number of client brochures and ads at our expense through the years because of typos and errors that should have been caught by proper proofreading. Often these errors occurred because the proofreader was the writer, who is the worst person for the task. The writer often will see what he "meant" to write.

The lesson learned has been translated into our agency policy— someone other than the writer must proof the copy, preferably out loud with another person. And after corrections are made, proofread it again. Even then, mistakes occur.

Experience has taught me to develop a doubtful mind when it comes to proofing copy. As we mentioned in Chapter VII, even a tiny comma can cause trouble, as in the joke about the definition of a Panda as a "large black-and-white, bear-like animal native to China. Eats, shoots and leaves."

In proofreading, as in all marketing today, you must consider the Internet impact. Proofreading has become even more crucial in the Internet-age because "netspeak" is creeping into copy.

The Internet and Marketing Language

E-mail and online texting, plus the ubiquity of blogs, Facebook, and Twitter, have led to a language revolution—the creation of "netspeak," a stylistic shorthand or slang. Basically, it substitutes letters, numbers, and keyboard symbols for sounds and words, such as "C" for "see," allowing users to communicate more quickly when their fingers are doing the talking. Acronyms have become an integral part of computer conversations. Today, you'll even find online dictionaries of this "Net Lingo." You'll also find it in marketing copy, most often written by younger practitioners, who get used to the slang in everyday personal communications. Worse yet, this slang has become acceptable English in some venues. If you can believe it, I read that one U.S. school district is accepting text messaging shorthand as correct spelling in school assignments.

In catching such slang in copy, as with typos, computer programs' spelling checkers are helpful, but they don't negate proofreading.

There's a long poem that for years has playfully cautioned against relying on spelling checkers. The first two stanzas of the original "spell checker poem" make the point:

I have a spelling checker
It came with my PC
It highlights for my review
Mistakes I cannot sea.

I ran this poem thru it
I'm sure your pleased to no
Its letter perfect in it's weigh
My checker told me sew.

But netspeak's impact on marketing can be much greater than spelling errors. If your reader/customer has to translate your language to understand it, you may create a barrier to your brand. The use of this shorthand can be difficult to comprehend if you're not used to it. You might figure out that *$ stands for Starbucks and "121" means "one-to-one." But how many of the uninitiated would understand that "GAFYK" means "get away from your keyboard" or "GI" stands for "Google it" not the soldier of World War II?

While the "new" language of Internet communications does not follow good writing standards for spelling and grammar, it's not necessarily negative or a dumbing down of written language.

Language is constantly changing and expanding. For example, in 2009, the Oxford New American Dictionary added "unfriend" as its word of the year. The impact of the Internet is clear: "unfriend" is a verb meaning to remove someone as a "friend" on a social network site such as Facebook.

So, the point of this discussion is not just about the value of proofreading or the intrusion of netspeak—it's about the mistake of not understanding their impact on our ability to communicate with the customer.

The Wax Museum and Other Errors

There are far bigger marketing mistakes than poor proofreading, and I have made some doozies; for example, making mistakes that cause business failure. Such was the case of the Annapolis Naval Historical Wax Museum, a project I helped develop back in the 1970s in an old A&P grocery store building on the City Dock in Annapolis, Maryland.

My partners and I, being local "experts" (we thought), assumed that the supposed one million tourists visiting Annapolis annually in those days would give us ample customers for this museum of latex figures depicting scenes of naval and local history. While we visited other wax museums and their creators to get marketing tips, we really didn't do our local homework well enough, and the museum failed to draw enough customers to meet its expenses. When we did our homework, after the fact, we discovered the million visitors was overstated, and a good portion of them, many from nearby Baltimore and Washington, D.C., came to Annapolis time and time again. A wax museum is not like a movie theater, where the show changes on a regular basis, attracting the same customers over and over. A wax museum like ours was static, never changing. If you've seen it once, there's little reason to return, we were told in customer interviews. Also, when you could visit the nearby U.S. Naval Academy and see John Paul Jones' crypt and the Academy's Navy museum, you were less likely to see value in a Naval historical wax museum. Expensive lesson learned: Don't do marketing research by the seat of your pants.

So, with a failed wax museum on our hands, what came next? Our "better late than never" homework on tourists coming to town showed us what we should have known in the first place. We found that the one thing almost all visitors did in Annapolis—whether they came for water sports, visiting historic buildings, seeing the Naval Academy, or just dining in the many restaurants—was to go shopping.

So, we turned the wax museum into a mini mall with great success. That was more than 35 years ago, and the mini mall is still going strong.

Much larger and more sophisticated companies have made similar errors. Take the Ford Motor Company's classic product mistake, the Edsel. In the early 1950s, Ford conducted various research studies on what was needed to close its competitive gap with General Motors. One market study concluded that Ford needed a new car for the young executive, but top level executives disagreed, saying that instead of a new car, Ford needed a whole new division with its own dealer network, and the company proceeded to develop it.

When they decided to name this division, Ford again drew on market research and commissioned public and employee surveys to get suggestions. It even asked poetess Marianne Moore to come up with names. With 6,000 names to choose from, the Ford Executive Committee chose none of them. Instead, they chose the name at the suggestion of the board chairman: "Why don't we call it Edsel?" Edsel Ford was founder Henry Ford's only son. Though family members opposed the name, it was adopted.

The design of the Edsel car was similarly flawed, though the original version was dramatic and different. By the time it was adjusted to fit various opinions and concessions, it was not much different than other auto designs of the 1950s.

Among the other errors that doomed the Edsel was Ford's introduction of the Fairlane in 1956, undercutting the Edsel's market, selling for less than the Edsel and, therefore, considered by many Ford buyers as a better value. After three years of production and limited sales, Ford killed the Edsel.

The marketing lesson of the Edsel was summed up by Anthony Young, an automotive historian, writing for the Foundation for Economic Education:

"The Edsel serves as a textbook example of corporate presumption and disregard for market realities. It also proved that advertising and pre-delivery hype have their limits in inducing consumers to buy a new and unproven car. In a free market economy, it is the car-buying public, not the manufacturer, that determines the success or failure of an automobile. A manufacturer cannot oversell a new car, or unrealistic expectations will be built up in the minds of consumers. If the newly introduced car doesn't live up to their expectations, it is practically doomed on the showroom floor.

"Ford learned from the Edsel that it couldn't dictate to consumers what they should buy. It hasn't made a similar mistake since. Several years after the Edsel's demise, Ford introduced the Mustang, a brand-new, sporty, affordable car Americans eagerly embraced. More recently, Ford introduced the Taurus, which was in response to the car buyer's needs and wants, and it has proved a tremendous market success. The Edsel will remain an automotive oddity—the answer to a question nobody asked."

Unlike the Edsel's disregard for customer needs and wants, the Coca Cola Company thought it was responding to customers when it introduced what was unofficially called "New Coke." Again, competitive forces drove the product change. In the 1970s, Pepsi had created a new brand image, a new presentation (bigger bottle), and new pricing promotions that cut into Coke's market share. Of course, Coke fought back with mammoth marketing programs, but the big stumbling block that kept coming up was taste.

Coke always prided itself on its "secret formula," but in research headed by the Coca-Cola marketing vice president Sergio Zyman, taste tests revealed that consumers preferred the sweeter taste of Pepsi. The marketing department then went into the field with a new, sweeter formulation of Coke. The results of the new taste test were a consumer preference for the new formulation over both regular Coke and Pepsi. Focus groups and surveys asked consumers if they would buy the new drink if it *were* Coca-Cola. Most said yes, though a minority, about 10-12 percent, were angered by the thought that Coke would change its vaunted formula—a clue to what would follow.

In 1985, the new Coke was introduced with "New!" on its containers. Despite New Coke's acceptance by the majority of Coca-Cola drinkers, a vocal minority damned the change. Coca-Cola's Atlanta headquarters began receiving angry calls and letters—some 400,000 of them. Newspaper columnists and comedians condemned or made light of the switch. Ads for New Coke were booed when they appeared on the scoreboard at the Houston Astrodome. Even Cuban dictator Fidel Castro, a longtime Coke drinker, criticized New Coke as a sign of American Capitalist decadence.

Within three months of New Coke's introduction, Coca Cola announced a return to the original formula and renamed it "Coca-Cola Classic," which later again became just "Coke."

Coca-Cola executives concluded that their mistake had been under-estimating the impact on its customer base, part of which had been alienated by the switch.

The whole episode, especially the switch back to the old Coke for-mula, had a dramatic marketing effect. It repositioned the brand in such a distinctive way that a Coke renaissance ensued. What had been per-ceived as a mistake, ultimately was a boon to sales.

While New Coke is most frequently mentioned now, as I have, as a cautionary tale against tampering with a well-established brand, it also presents some positive marketing lessons. In his book, *The End of Marketing As We Know It*, former Coke marketing executive Sergio Zyman says the mistakes made in developing New Coke "turned out to be a roaring success for Coca-Cola, because it rekindled the relationship between the American public and Classic Coke."

"But," he adds, "the only reason it wasn't a disaster is that we were willing to learn from the experience and to change our minds."

Therein lies a basic premise of this chapter, be willing to learn from your mistakes. If your ad campaign isn't working, that doesn't mean you should stop advertising. As you can see, the most successful businesses make mistakes. The key is to learn from your marketing mistakes so you don't repeat the same error in the future.

Of course, the biggest blunder is not keeping your eye on the cus-tomer. It's the one mistake that could be fatal.

That's the basic premise of this book. Never forget, the customer *IS* your business, as I learned from my experience and many mentors, as in:

"Marketing . . . is not a specialized activity at all," said Peter Drucker, "It is the whole business seen from the point of view of its final result; that is, from the customer's point of view."

Suggested Reading

American Brands Council. 'America's Greatest Brands; Volume IV' (2005). America's Greatest Brands, Inc.

Beckwith, Harry. 'Selling the Invisible: A Field Guide to Modern Marketing' (1997). Warner Books, Inc.

Blankenship, A.B. and Breen, George Edward. 'State of the Art Marketing Research' (1993). NTC Publishing Group.

Drucker, Peter F. 'The Practice of Management' (1954, 1982, 1986). HarperBusiness.

Fallon, Pat and Senn, Fred. 'Juicing the Orange: How to Turn Creativity into a Powerful Business Advantage' (2006). Harvard Business School Press.

Freiberg, Kevin and Freiberg, Jackie. 'NUTS: Southwest Airlines' Crazy Recipe for Business and Personal Success' (1996). Broadway Books.

Hanan, Mack and Karp, Peter. 'Customer Satisfaction: How to Maximize, Measure and Market Your Company's "Ultimate Product" ' (1991). American Management Association.

Kermally, Sultan. 'Gurus on Marketing' (2003). Thorogood.

Kotler, Philip and Andreasen, Alan. 'Strategic Marketing for Nonprofit Organizations, Fourth Edition' (1991). Prentice-Hall.

Kotler, Philip and Armstrong, Gary. 'Principles of Marketing: Fifth Edition' (1991). Prentice-Hall.

Peters, Tom. 'The Pursuit of WOW' (1994). Macmillan.

Peters, Thomas and Waterman, Robert H., Jr. 'In Search of Excellence' (2004, 1982). HarperCollins.

Ries, Al and Trout, Jack. 'Positioning: The Battle for Your Mind' (2001). McGraw-Hill.

Schultz, Don E., Tannenbaum, Stanley I. and Lauterborn, Robert F. 'Integrated Marketing Communications' (1994). NTC/Contemporary Publishing Group.

Scott, David Meerman. 'The New Rules of Marketing & PR' (2007). John Wiley & Sons, Inc.

Stone, Bob. 'Successful Direct Marketing Methods' (1997). NTC/Contemporary Publishing Group.

Woolf, Brian P. 'Customer Specific Marketing: The New Power in Retailing' (1996). Cadmus Publishing.

Zyman, Sergio and Miller, Scott. 'Building Brandwidth: Closing the Sale Online' (2000). HarperCollins.

Zyman, Sergio. 'The End of Marketing As We Know It' (1999). HarperBusiness.